THE TRIUMPH OF PRESBYTERIANISM

THE TRIUMPH OF PRESBYTERIANISM

WILLIAM M. CAMPBELL
B.D., Ph.D., D.Litt.

THE SAINT ANDREW PRESS
EDINBURGH

©
WILLIAM M. CAMPBELL
1958

PRINTED IN SCOTLAND BY
ROBERT CUNNINGHAM AND SONS LTD., ALVA

To my wife
to my father and mother
and to the late Dr J. D. Ogilvie of Milngavie
to all of whom this book owes so much
I dedicate it

CONTENTS

INTRODUCTION

In 1638, Scotland established the Presbyterian form of Church government in her national Church. Political, social and economic conditions, as well as the ecclesiastical situation, combined to effect this reformation, for Scottish affairs show a great complexity of motive and a greater variety of character as the ruder age of the reiver gives way to the political age of the Reformation. The predatory baron is still there, but evangelist, agitator, pamphleteer, politician, scholar, lawyer, burgher and divine all play their part in shaping events and dictating policies. Despite ambition and intrigue, there is more honesty of purpose and finer loyalties on both sides than has ever been seen before in contending Scottish factions. The men who signed the National Covenant believed that the Presbyterian order was that most assuredly set forth in God's word, that it was the most free and best suited to the Scottish nation and that its establishment was God's will in their time. Historians seldom write of this time with impartiality. A present fashion is to vilify the Covenanters, as a past fashion was to blackguard Charles, James and Claverhouse. Vile and stupid cruelties were perpetrated by both sides but in the present age, we have bloodily seen too much of the *lex talionis* to be harshly critical of our ancestors. Tyrannies are not overcome without blood; freedom is not won without tears, nor is it kept without sweat.

The National Covenant which abolished the Episcopate was the climax to the strife between Episcopacy and Presbyterianism for establishment as the national form of Church government. Professor G. D. Henderson, following Pannier, holds that the strictures of the Reformers were not so much directed against the bishop's office as against his 'tyranny' due to the prelatic development of the primitive ideal. But this does not take the matter far enough, in the case of the Covenanters not nearly far enough. Alexander Henderson and his supporters certainly objected to the tyranny of the bishop; they objected also to his being a tool of the Crown and a toady to the nobility—though there were bishops who were neither tyrants, tools nor toadies, and Presbyterians who, beginning as truculent demagogues, ended as sycophantic careerists in the Protector's ante-rooms. They objected *in toto* to the bishops because they *were* bishops. To overlook this is to ignore the teaching of Andrew Melville and the opposition to the bishop's office as early as 1574, to ignore the appeal which the doctrine of parity of ministers made to the Scots, to ignore the spiritual instinct which made them insist on a common table as well as a common cup, and to ignore the torrent of tomes and tractates in the sixteenth and seventeenth centuries poured out to prove the bishop's office utterly unscriptural in any other sense than that held by the Presbyterian and Puritan. In 1638 the Bishops were 'outed'—and most vindictively excommunicated—both because of what they were and of what they did. Henderson wrote a pamphlet styled *Certain Reasons tending to prove the Unlawfulness of all Diocesan Episcopacy, even the most moderate.* Others wrote more in a similar strain, with less restraint. Whenever in subsequent negotiations on uniformity of Church government the matter of non-prelatic Episcopacy was even hinted at, the Scots reacted with the horror of an escaped Trojan for the wooden horse and set up the doctrine of the divine right of Presbyterian Church government as an iron gate against the bishops' return.

The old controversy is again with us, with all the old fears and all the old arguments. Bishops are opposed because they may become 'bossy', pompous and clique-ridden. Grave and reasonable doubts are expressed as to whether 'bishops in Presbytery' would add efficiency to the Church and the argument based on efficiency is very tenuous, for to balance the standards of efficiency in the Anglican and Presbyterian systems would be a complicated and exasperating process. Few Scotsmen, scholars or laymen, will accept the doctrine of Apostolic Succession and any attempted fusion of it with the idea of the continuity of the faithful brings only confusion. This leaves the achievement of 'unity' as the great argument for the re-introduction of bishops into the Church of Scotland, but the historian may well question if an obtruded alteration in Church government is the best way to secure an integral and spiritual unity and if the new objection may not be that the bishops are being 'stuck in', just as one of the old objections was that they were 'stuck up'.

It is no new thing for Scotsmen to be ecumenically minded. Henderson and the early Covenanters deplored division: the idea of the one true Church was ever in their hearts and minds and they sought to abolish the things which divided—bishops in the Anglican Church particularly. When they came to Westminster, the Scots found the bishops gone and they settled down with the English Puritans to frame the standards of doctrine, worship and government which were to unite the Churches of both nations. Much of what was framed was a triumph for the persuasive and intellectual powers of the Scots, but the rise of Cromwell and the return of Charles prevented the work of the Westminster Assembly effecting any settled result in the matter of Church union. Would it have done so, even if political circumstances had been favourable? A study of the history of this time may raise the pertinent question as to whether unity is to be found either in the elimination or the introduction of a specific component in the life of the Church. It can be noted that even when the components differed, the early Reformers, Puritan, Anglican, Presbyterian, and Independent could sit at one Communion table.

There exists still in the Church the age-old and deep-seated antithesis of puritan and liturgist, democrat and authoritarian; usually, though there are varying degrees of the combination, the puritan is linked with the democrat, the liturgist with the authoritarian. We all seek the form of worship and government we want and seek in Scripture the text or interpretation which supports them, and the new scholarship can be found using the arguments of text selection as robustly and repeatedly as the old scholasticism. It is not proposed to enter the controversy here. I cannot find that Jesus dogmatised about any way of worship except that it should be sincere, still less that he dogmatised about any way of government. Paul, as translated by the Authorised Version, talks of Christians keeping the 'unity of the spirit in the bond of peace'. In a right interpretation and practice of these words, the Church might find the oneness it seeks.

It had been the original intention to call this book *The Second Reformation in Scotland*, but perhaps *The Triumph of Presbyterianism* more truly represents its content, not because it was the triumph of Presbyterianism over Episcopacy, but because it saw the emergence of Presbyterianism as a clearly defined order of Church government, with far-reaching consequences for Scotland, and, through the triumph of Scottish thought in framing the Westminster standards of government, still further consequences in the moulding of the later Presbyterian Churches. Though their faults are not concealed, I have tried to see the leading protagonists as children of their age, an age too complex to be seen in terms of black and white. If the biographical chapters show here and there a little redundancy, they will show how the same events shape the mind and character of men totally different in nature and temperament, but devoted to one cause. Of their passionate sincerity there can be no doubt, for, much as they sought unity, they sought truth more. It had to be a true unity: the phrases 'the true Church', the 'true form of Church government', the 'true faith', are forever on the lips of these men who were by turn far-sighted and short-sighted, patient and impatient, arrogant and humble, disciplined and undisciplined in their terrible search for truth. The early Covenanters were devoted men and great scholars. They have to be restored to their place in the making of modern Scotland.

CHAPTER I

THE RESURGENCE
OF PRESBYTERIANISM

THE SIGNING of the National Covenant and the political and religious upheaval which followed it were events, not only of national, but of international importance, for the triumph of the Presbyterian cause had far reaching effects outside Scotland and beyond the seventeenth century. At the same time it must be remembered that, despite some political manoeuvre and manipulation, the triumph sprang out of the social, religious and political needs and aspirations of the Scottish people. This chapter will endeavour to underline these facts.

Professor Hume Brown has said, 'Calvinism by the characters which it formed saved Protestantism in Europe, and with equal truth it may be said that Presbyterianism saved it in Scotland.' But Presbyterianism in Scotland did not survive without a grim struggle. Knox triumphed over Mary, but Morton and a rapacious nobility wrecked his finest plans. Melville triumphed in 1592, only to have all that he had won for a Presbyterian Church filched and forced from her grasp by the astute James VI. The Union of the Crowns saw James already well on the way to establish Episcopacy in Scotland and, when he was safely enthroned as ruler of both kingdoms, all his added power was used to establish Episcopacy both in discipline and in ritual in the Northern Kingdom. But the hatred of Romanism was so much bound up with the ritual question that when his son sought to follow out James's policy to its ultimate conclusion, the popular reaction drove bishops and all their appurtenances out of Scotland. Thus the years 1625-52 saw the struggle for and the establishment of the Presbyterian Church system at which Melville had aimed. Moreover it was so established that even the temporary imposition of a supine Episcopacy under Charles II could not displace it from the hearts of the people nor from the ultimate political framework of the Revolution Settlement in Scotland, which by Act of Parliament disestablished Episcopacy because it was 'contrary to the will of the generality of the people'.

It can be said with some truth that Scotland owes her Church and her national individuality and character to the men who fought for religious and political freedom against the monarchic despotism which had subdued, first by force, then by bribery, the bulk of the feudal nobility into being tools of the Crown. Historical conjecture is dangerous, but what would have been the fate of the two countries had Scottish Presbyterianism *not* triumphed in 1638? If Charles had obtained his ends in Scotland, with Scotland quiet, he might have equally easily won in England, for the Scots entered the Civil War when Parliament's fortunes were at their lowest ebb and greatly helped to save the Parliamentary cause. They as much as, if the truth be told, possibly more than Cromwell, won Marston Moor, and, but for them, Charles I might have achieved a speedy victory in England. Later his sons, the one with his secret, the other with his avowed, bent to Roman Catholicism, might have gradually, or even decidedly, re-established that faith on a cowed nation. James certainly would have done so had he had the power.

In the early seventeenth century, the danger seemed even more acute to the Protestant than in the days of Titus Oates, for the Thirty Years' War was raging and there were strong Roman Catholic parties in both Kingdoms. The establishment of Presbyterianism in 1638 certainly prevented Scotland from having Episcopacy as her national Church system. But it did more: it saved her from being an ecclesiastical hatchery or forcing-ground where a monarch could try out his innovations (as Charles and Laud sought to do) before imposing them on the Southern Kingdom. Had Charles I succeeded with Episcopacy, James II and Charles II might well have experimented in Scotland as to how far they could go with Roman Catholicism, and in saving Scotland from an arbitrarily imposed Episcopacy, the Covenant leaders may have saved both Kingdoms from any despotic re-establishment of the ancient Church.

The second thing of note about the triumph of Presbyterianism is that though it was halted by Cromwell and though, as a system, it was never established in England, yet from the work of the Presbyterians between the years 1630 and 1652 the great Presbyterian Churches of the world have sprung. It was the Scots who, as we shall see, defined Presbyterianism in England and helped to give it form and order. The Westminster Assembly gave an English Calvinism to Scotland but it gave a predominantly Scottish Presbyterian ideal to England. On the Westminster standards the Presbyterian Churches have been founded and had the Scots not taken part at Westminster, something quite different would have emerged. When we look, therefore, to the Presbyterian Churches in England, U.S.A., Canada and South Africa, we can certainly say that they are what they are because of the success of the Scottish National Covenant—and of that much maligned second covenant, the Solemn League and Covenant.

Perhaps most immediately important of all is the fact that the establishment of Presbyterianism was a national movement and as nearly a democratic movement as anything brought forth till the Reform Bill. James VI had established his way by despotism —as far as James was concerned, for ordinary folks in Scotland a benevolent despotism. Cunning, canny, even treacherous, he was a lover of peace and did seek prosperity for his 'ain folk', to the disgust of his English subjects. Despite Presbyterian opposition, James had won his way because he had in Scotland the queer popularity of the man who is laughed at but tolerated, and even liked. The burghers sensed that he wished them well, knew his desire to further their commercial and industrial interests, so they accepted a moderate Episcopacy, perhaps as a *quid pro quo* for his good intentions. The barons accepted it quite readily because they still enjoyed all the spoils of the Church. The one class least inclined to accept was the smaller country laird who had no great share of the kirk spoils, no great interest in trade, suffered not a few economic burdens and had nothing done in his interests.

The leading Reformation ministers of this time, Bruce, Boyd, Henderson, Rutherford, Douglas and many more all came from this class. Under James, the desire for a more democratic religion and for social justice along with the desire of the countryman for fuller say in national affairs was kept in check. Then came Charles, who made at least two political blunders which united baron, burgher and laird all against him and gave every class in the country a hand in the National Covenant so that Scotsmen had never been so nationally minded since the War of Independence.

This period, then, saw the swift decline of Roman Catholicism in Scotland. It was the period which established Presbyterianism in the form in which it is now known in many lands and in this period the struggle to achieve these things made Scotland more of a nation than she had been for many years.

What of the immediate significance? Was there a real need for a 'Reformation'? Could Scotland not have been evangelised and educated and have grown in national character under Episcopacy? To deal with the last first, it was clearly apparent to many Scotsmen of the time that the more Episcopal Scotland became, the more provincial became her destiny. The Scottish bishops had to accept Episcopal ordination in England in 1612. Though this was given by other bishops than those of York and Canterbury, in order that Archbishop Spottiswood's national susceptibilities might not be offended or the superiority of York and Canterbury over St. Andrews implied, yet subsequently Laud's whole attitude towards Scotland was that of a man seeking, through useful agents, to subjugate a rude, recalcitrant, provincial Church. The more her Church conformed to English practice, the less of a nation Scotland became. Gradually Scotsmen became aware of this, and it seemed to them that a second Reformation was needed that Scotland might have a Church order of her own as an expression of her own predilections in doctrine, discipline and worship, and none expressed this more finely and clearly than Robert Boyd, Principal of Glasgow University. Such a Church order had to be freely chosen without any compulsion or direction by England and alone could express the national character and spiritual aspirations. The National Covenant which established it was a necessary declaration of national, political and spiritual independence, for by 1638 we needed our own Church to be our own nation.

How had the 'tulchanate' of James VI fulfilled its duties towards the people of Scotland? It is not fair to blame its members entirely for their failures. The Church revenues from which Knox had hoped to evangelise, educate and hospitalise Scotland had been used by James, with amazing success, as bribes to keep his barons placid and pliable. The higher and more important clergy secured a certain competence; the lesser clergy were in many parishes ill-paid, or unpaid, and in others there were none at all. Despite legislation for its erection, the parish school was not anything like widespread, whole areas were without law, letters or any approach to the religious life. The pages of Calderwood and the Records of the Assemblies are full of accounts of the ignorance, immorality and backsliding of the people, the lawlessness of the lairds and the lack of 'guid and godly' men to bring about a better state of affairs. Calderwood, the Presbyterian historian, may have been only too glad to lay the blame for this state of affairs on the Episcopal regime, but life at this time was often nasty, brutish and short, and the Episcopate, with the possible exception of the area round Aberdeen, did little to improve matters, perhaps because they could do little. In 1636 Charles I himself rebuked the bishops for their remissness in failing to plant schools in the parishes, which had been ordered by the Privy Council in 1616 and enjoined by Parliament in 1633. One quotation from Calderwood will suffice to show that the gospel was marching with somewhat leaden feet. 'An exceeding great grief to behold the true word of God contemptuously despised by the great multitude, sacraments profaned, the discipline of the Kirk set nothing by . . . for what part of the land is not aspate with the abusing of the blessed name of God, with swearing, lies, perjury, with mercats, gluttony, drunkenness, fighting, playing, dancing, with rebelling against magistrates, with blood taking,

B

incest, fornication and adultery.' The Episcopate had been unable to do much in the way of moral reformation because they had not the staff and some of them little of the zeal to do it. Under Presbyterian rule, the task was attempted more successfully. Mistakes were made, even gross mistakes, like the parish witch-hunts or the Act of Classes, a political 'witch-hunt'; discipline was severe and zeal could deteriorate into hypocrisy, but Scotland was given an evangelical faith by men with a zeal for propagating it, a faith which penetrated into every corner and which took the gospel and the school everywhere. Scotland was made more civilised by Presbyterianism. Despite the sneer that the Church imposed only an external decency, it was by the Presbyterian minister and teacher that the rudeness and the crudeness of the feudal age was finally broken, even as James VI had broken its political power. None can pretend that a few years after the Covenant Scotland enjoyed the golden age that Kirkton, the historian, elaborates. But far more was achieved than detracting historians allow. Schools and kirks were planted. The work was begun on a solid foundation and the Revolution gave the Kirk peace to consolidate part of what Knox had visualised and the Covenanter begun to achieve.

In the early seventeenth century the desire for a doctrinal teaching standardised in form and content, and for a stabilised and orderly form of worship was strong among both Episco-palians and Presbyterians. They differed, of course, regarding the method of achievement, but the innovations of James, the intran-sigence of Charles, the advent of Arminianism and later of New England Puritanism, widened their differences and turned acad-emic animosities into bitter hate and strife. Scotland was Pro-testant; those who knew what these words meant were Presby-terian or Episcopalian, but there were many who knew only that they were anti-Romanist. As far as catechetical teaching was concerned, various catechisms had been printed. Calvin's in 1564, the Little Catechism, the Palatine Catechism, Craig's Catechism, Davidson's Catechism all followed. Adams and Pont had each a Latin metrical catechism. There were sundry other catechetical forms in print and English catechisms were not unknown. But even with this variety, circulation was limited, for printing was limited. The old Scots Confession of Faith was still known and revered, and a new Confession of Faith, drafted by Hall and John Adamson and approved by the Assembly of 1616, was suspect to the Presbyterians because of an article affirming the belief that the Church of Scotland (apparently as then established) was one of the most pure Kirks under heaven, although it was as ortho-doxly Calvinist as its predecessor. But as time went on, with two competing systems of Church government and the beginning of two competing systems of theology, the early seventeenth century in Scotland saw a sort of catechetical chaos and a desire for a standardised teaching which ultimately produced the Westminster standards.

Knox's Book of Common Order of 1564 had long been the Church's directory of Worship. How much it was followed by 1620-30, it is difficult to say. It was almost certainly used with variations to suit the views or the needs or the deficiencies of the officiating minister. So much so, that James VI and Charles I on the one hand, and Alexander Henderson and the Covenanters on the other, sought to have it superseded. One need not discuss the merits and demerits of the Book of Common Order as com-pared with the other directories and liturgies. What emerges is that there was a desire for and a need for reform by establishing, as well as basic doctrinal teaching, a regular and authoritative form of public worship. James and Charles sought to impose an unwanted form. Scotland took her own and, by a strange turn of fortune, hammered it out for herself in that very stronghold and sanctuary of the King and Church who sought to impose an alien form upon them.

Protestantism has frequently been the champion of the political liberties of man, and especially Calvinist and Presbyterian Pro-testantism. In Scotland there was some need of a political revolu-tion. James boasted in England, 'This I must say for Scotland and may truly vaunt it. Here I sit and govern it with my pen, I write and it is done and by a clerk of Council I govern Scotland now—

which others could not do with the sword.' By a series of administrative changes in conduct of Parliamentary affairs, by handpicking his officials, by bribing his barons, James governed Scotland at his own whim. The exile of Melville, the imprisonment of ministers in Blackness, the pacification of the unruly Borders, the abolition of General Assemblies—the only Parliament where men could speak freely—the destruction of the Clan Gregor, the commencement of social improvement in the Highlands, the Plantation of Ulster, the imposition of the Perth Articles, the encouragement of trade and industry, all these, good and ill, were carried through by the will of James and the instrumentality of his agents and Crown officers. Hume Brown considers the years 1603 to 1623 the years in which Scottish Monarchy came nearest to despotism. The barons, who in old days had limited it, were now its servants. The King had the power of the purse. The Church was crushed and subservient, or appeared so. The burgher enjoyed a security he had not known before and the measure of prosperity that went with it, so was not likely to question his power. The lesser lairds had little voice save to assent in Parliament to the decisions of the King's men. There was need of the free voice of Scotsmen to be heard to save her nationhood, to save her Parliament from becoming a King's committee—hardly even that—and her Kirk from becoming an appanage of the State.

One may end this chapter with a biographical note to link the age of Andrew Melville with the age of Samuel Rutherfurd. How was the Presbyterianism of Andrew Melville kept alive and handed on to those who perfected his work? Till the day of his death, Andrew Melville was in constant correspondence with Scotland. It is impossible here to evaluate his work and in his own lifetime he saw little result of it except frustration. It cannot be affirmed that the policy of the Second Book of Discipline had ever thoroughgoing effect till after 1638. But Melville imparted both his policy and his spirit to the men who came after him. He was a man of outstanding courage. He had dared the barons —'bangsters' he called them when they sought to break the discipline of Glasgow College—and made them look extremely foolish. He had thwarted James VI and made him look foolish— a thing James never forgave. To James, Melville was the incarnate symbol of the Kirk's resistance to the State in all its efforts to control her destiny. The later Reformers departed in some ways from his policy, never from his leading principle of free decision in the affairs of God's house which they held forth in their doctrine of Christ's Headship of the Church, and when the National Covenant was signed in 1638, the spirit of those who brought it into being was that of Andrew Melville living on through his friends and disciples. Of these friends and disciples, the one who lived long enough to see the embers of Presbyterianism blowing to a flame again was Robert Bruce. He was the man who most kept Melville's principles alive for the succeeding age and imparted his spirit to Henderson, Dickson, Rutherfurd, Gillespie and those who came after.

Robert Bruce strides with the full stride of a man from the robust age of Mary to the polemic age of the Covenant. He filled Knox's pulpit in St. Giles' but he was, we are told, no Boanerges. As resolute as Melville, but without his bitter vehemence, he walks, serious and dour, through a stormy age of violence with all the patient firmness of purpose of his great ancestor. Like the Bruce, he never gave up his cause, and like him, he made even exile bring forth fruit. He could remember the murder of Riccio and Darnley. He was almost adult when Moray and Lennox both died of violence. The maiden had but fallen on Morton, when he gave himself to the service of the Kirk. He was appointed to St. Giles' in the year of Mary's execution. He lost his charge because he would not believe a king's account of a political assassination. He lived in ecclesiastical exile for twenty-six years and did more for Scottish Protestantism in exile than he achieved from the great Kirk of St. Giles. He was the man who showed the Presbyterian ministry how to combat the nobility's violence and the wiles of the monarchy by the patient and evangelical preaching of the Word in quiet places. The highlights of his life show what manner of man he was.

Bruce was the second son of Alexander Bruce of Airth, the usual baron of his age, greedy of land, generous to his kinsmen, murderous when thwarted. His mother was a bigoted Roman Catholic, an unpromising heritage for the saintliest and least ambitious of the Scottish Reformers. He was born about 1554 and we find him registered Bachelor in St. Andrews University in 1571 and Master in 1573. He proceeded from there to study law in the University of Louvain, which was strongly Romanist, and returned to Scotland to practise with a possible view to the College of Justice. In 1581 he became converted from formal Protestantism to a deeper faith and a dedicated service. Quiet and introspective by nature, his story of this event shows the vivid sense of the personal power of evil that we find in Luther, coupled with the passionate, decisive sincerity of Augustine. He tells us that, lying in bed one August evening, God quickened his conscience. 'He made the devil to accuse me so audibly that I heard his voice as vividly as ever I heard anything not being asleep but awake—Yea I was so fearfully and extremely tormented that I would have been content to have been cast into the cauldron of hot melted lead to have had my soul relieved of this unsupportable weight.' But he tells us that ere the day dawned or the sun rose, he found peace and gave himself to the work of Christ. He returned the lands of Kinnaird which his father had given him and set out to study theology in St. Andrews, the St. Andrews of Andrew and James Melville. He was to remain the lifelong friend and staunch supporter of these men in all the vicissitudes that were to follow. When Melville was tried for treason in 1584, Bruce stood by him. In 1587, the Assembly appointed him to St. Giles' where he preached first in the South Kirk and later in the Little Kirk. In February 1588, at the age of thirty-four, he was Moderator of the General Assembly which was 'extraordinarily convened for great dangers' (the Armada was imminent). It made an unflinching denunciation of the Catholic nobles who were acting as traitors to the realm, and for once James took the Kirk's advice and acted against them.

Less thunderous in utterance than Knox, he could quite caustically tell James to hold his tongue when his ill-mannered babbling disturbed the sermon. Yet James liked him as he never did Andrew Melville, and made him one of the Council which governed the country during his absence wooing Anne of Denmark. As the King became more and more set in the establishment of Episcopacy, the rift between the two men widened. Bruce was as great a Puritan as Knox and his criticisms of the conduct of the royal court made the young Queen his enemy. When James used the anti-Catholic riots of 1596 to break the Kirk's power, Bruce had to flee the town. The final break came with the Gowrie Plot. Bruce refused to believe James's account of the affair. He had what Calderwood calls a native obstinacy— and also a native scepticism—and James's account of the affair would make even the least sceptical smile. Many and bitter were the conferences between them. The King came to like Bruce's dry sarcasm as little as Melville's dogmatism, till, on one occasion, badgered beyond endurance by Bruce's cross-questioning him as to what happened, James replied, 'I had neither God nor devil before my eyes but my own defence.' Shortly before this, James had put humiliation on Bruce by insisting on his re-ordination owing to some irregularity in his first appointment. Bruce, in his Master's cause, had accepted that. He would accept no more. The formula on James's innocence which he signed did not please the King, so he was finally evicted from St. Giles' in 1605 and forbidden to preach.

It was then that his life's work bore its best fruit. Twice exiled to Inverness, he preached there. The rest of the time he spent journeying over central Scotland, a heroic, legendary figure from a great age. He was the real beginner of the Conventicle, as later known. To house and field, in small numbers and great, men came to hear him. He drew round him a band of men who were to evangelise southern Scotland and pave the way for the Covenant. His great ally was Robert Boyd, Principal of Glasgow University. His disciples, David Dickson, Robert Blair, John Livingstone and others went far and near over the south-west. But a greater than these heard the call. One Sunday in 1615,

Robert Bruce preached in the Kirk in Forgan and a young man, minister of Leuchars, well hidden at the back of the Kirk, heard him. As Sheriff Orr writes, 'Bruce's wandering ministry was a fruitful one but, judged by subsequent events, that Sunday in Forgan Kirk was his greatest hour. He won Alexander Henderson, one of the greatest fishes in his net.' When Bruce died in 1631, he had taken the torch from Knox and Melville, he had lit countless kirks in Scotland and he had placed it in the hands of Alexander Henderson.

Bruce's sermons were clear, lucid, evangelical, teaching sermons, full of good Scots idiom—the sermons of a man who did not find faith easy, for he was a canny man with a good deal of natural scepticism in his nature—as James found. He once said, 'I think it is a great matter to believe there is a God' and added that belief was something a great deal more difficult than people thought. Perhaps because of this he was always at pains to explain, but explain with great fervour. He was so much loved that a whole hagiology sprang up round his name. Andrew Melville called him 'That confessor, almost martyr, of the Lord Jesus'. John Livingstone said, 'No man since the apostles' time spoke with such power.' Crabbed David Calderwood exclaimed, 'Bruce may my soul at last be with thine.' Robert Bruce kept the lamp of Presbyterianism burning in Scotland in its early, darkest hour, even as his ancestor kept the lamp of independence lit.

CHAPTER II

PREPARATION FOR THE CONFLICT

THERE WERE certain factors, geographical and traditional, which were astutely used by the Presbyterians in the furtherance of their cause to provide the groundwork—or undergroundwork—of their success. One of the most vital of these was the ultra-Protestantism of south-west Scotland. In geographic position, Galloway and southern Ayrshire were remote and secluded, but not isolated. Early in the fifteenth century, the English Lollard, hunted from his Lancastrian home by the zealous and political orthodoxy of Henry V, and later of his son's 'Protectors', found an asylum in the glens of Galloway and the uplands of southern Ayrshire. The Solway crossing was an easy and quick escape. The Lollards of Kyle (1494), whatever their doctrines may or may not have been, give evidence of a stream of reforming thought trickling into Scotland through the bare Galloway hills. It is notable that those districts in which Lollardy gained strongest hold became subsequently most aggressively Protestant—for instance, south-western England which suffered most heavily under the Marian persecution and which, rising for Monmouth, suffered again in the 'Bloody Assize'. The track of land from southern Ayrshire to the coast between Wigtown and Kirkcudbright, the Lollard trail surely, became in an ultra-Presbyterian country, more than ultra-Presbyterian, the home of the Cameronian and the slaughterhouse of the dragoon. Wodrow preserves the fact that some of the lairds in that country, like Gordon of Airds, ancestor of the Kenmures, were traditionally Lollard.

The south-west also formed an asylum for the later Scottish Reformer. In the minority of Mary, it was the only safe one. North and west he could hardly go, for he spoke a strange tongue to the Gael. North-east he dare not go, for Huntly was Roman

Catholic and orthodox. So Kyle again resumes its role as a 'receptacle of the servants of God of old'. Wishart had fled to Ayrshire and preached there. Knox followed in the winter of 1556 and also in 1562, drawn no doubt by policy and sentiment. The first to defy the Queen Regent, to meddle with their preachers, was a band of Ayrshire lairds, direct descendants of the Lollards of Kyle, headed by Chalmers of Gaitgirth, a house still staunchly Presbyterian in the days of Rutherfurd. The political situation aided the geographic in keeping a reformist tradition alive in the south-west. The history of Scotland from 1400 to 1550 is a sordid story. No great social or even political movement can be seen in it, if one excepts James IV's attempts at a Renaissance and James V's at law reform, only a nobility obeying their own whim, in a search for power, or a grab for land, reckless of their own, their family's or their country's honour. Till the Reformation, which at least gave some of the nobles a common cause for which to fight, even if it was only for a common ecclesiastical purse to loot, internal politics are a vortex of feuds, jealousies and assassinations. The Scottish baron, as long as he had riders at his back, recked little what they believed. James V and Beaton when they stirred the fires of persecution only provoked a few sparks which burned and died upon themselves.

None of the south-western nobles distinguished themselves by their zeal for orthodoxy, or for Stewart loyalty. The relationship of the Stewarts with them is more than interesting. The old Douglas house, Lords of Galloway, had perished by the treachery of James II. The south-western nobles were responsible for the overthrow and assassination of James III. The 'Assured Scots' were mostly of the south-west and too near English gold for loyalty to the Scottish Crown. Holinshed quotes the Prior of Whithorn as agent in some dealing whereby all the gentlemen of Nithsdale, Galloway and Annandale came over to Henry's party. What religious views the greater nobles such as Cassillis and Glencairn had, were inclined to the reformed doctrines current in England. For the lesser, raiding, not religion, was their preoccupation. The Wicliffite, and later the Reformed wheat

flourished here and there in the south-west because of its conceal-
ment amongst so much armed thistle. Stewart orthodoxy found
few to sponsor it here, and there is little or no record of religious
persecution. What tentative support their self-interest allowed,
the nobles gave to the Reformed preacher. Maxwell, Catholic
though he was, moved in Parliament that the Bible be read in the
vernacular. The Douglases, to oppose Beaton, lent an ear, and
Cassillis and Glencairn, both of them to the Reformed doctrine,
especially as preached by Sir Ralph Sadleyr, who was, as Lang
says, very ready to suborn to the glory of God. The lairds
followed their overlords.

There were thus certain pre-natal conditions which favoured
the birth and growth of Presbyterian Protestantism in the south-
west. Except when a portion of the lairds won thereto by Maxwell supported Mary at Langside, their policy is consistently
Protestant. The First Book of Discipline was signed by most of
the south-western peers and barons, Glencairn, Maxwell, Drum-
lanrig, Lochinvar, Garlies and Bargany, the lesser lairds and
barons of Galloway being again in preponderance amongst their
kind in support of the reformed faith. The Band of Ayr (1562)
(Glencairn, Loudon, Gaitgirth, Dalrymple, Fergushill) shows
united adhesion to the cause. Langside only temporarily detached
Lochinvar. In 1574 came the first hint that the opposition to
Papacy would now in the south-west transfer itself to opposition
to Episcopacy. John Davidson, tried for his book *Dialogue of a
Clerk and a Courtier*, withdrew to Rusco in the parish of Anwoth,
a house of Lochinvar. The gentlemen of the west failed to get
him pardoned and he was exiled. From then until the Bishops'
Wars, with the exception of the Johnstone-Maxwell feud, the
south-west remained politically quiet.

Quiet, but not dead, for despite the strong hand of Morton and
the cunning hand of James which had kept the nobles thirled to
their Erastian Church policy, a more evangelical religion was
preached and flourished in many a small country town like Ayr
or Kirkcudbright and in many a laird's house. Robert Bruce and
his friends found a ready welcome. Then came Charles who

made the first political mistake which united all classes against him. It was only a 'political' mistake for the measure proposed was sound and well-intentioned. Nevertheless, it was a 'mistake' which, as much as 'Laud's Liturgy', gave us a Presbyterian Scotland. Laud roused Scotland to assert itself, but Charles's Act of Revocation had already evangelised her and made the south-west his resolute and determined opponent. The 'mistake' was the Act of Revocation of 1625. By it Charles sought to revoke the grants of much of the Church's land and property with which his father had bribed the barons and gentry—or which the Regents had apportioned to their followers. He offered a fair compensation—if paid—but not a compensation apportionate to the loss. His object was good in that it was to be put to ecclesiastical purposes, and especially to augment the minimum stipends which were little more than pittances, if that. Of course a good deal of the land was to find its way back to the Episcopal sees. The result was that the nobles and gentry became, for very patent and material motives, thirstily Presbyterian. The Act of Revocation destroyed the Episcopate which it was meant to serve. Charles pleased nobody but the Bishops and from now, all parties of the State, except the Bishops, verged slowly into a coalition against him. The immediate effect was that Presbyterian propaganda and preaching now enjoyed greater freedom and encouragement than at any time since 1590. The greater nobles, distrusting its democratic savour, had never (with a few exceptions) warmly supported the Presbyterian faith on its own merit. They had been content with the Episcopal or semi-Episcopal establishment of James VI, especially as they still enjoyed the ecclesiastical rents and teinds. Their opposition to the Anglicanism of Charles was largely due to the fact that it involved sooner or later a re-division of ecclesiastical plunder; they would vehemently oppose any church except one which they could starve. Now begins a scurrying for 'guid and godly' men to fill their parishes and uproot all things Episcopal, men who like Rutherfurd would be unworldly enough to be content with 300 marks stipend, instead of 800. The common folk of the Midlands and the Lowlands had hitherto been more anti-Romanist than ultra-Presbyterian. From this time they were to be proselytised and evangelised as never before. The 'Stewarton sickness' was to infect many parishes in the land. The former popular zeal against idols was to be re-directed by Charles's folly and Presbyterian policy against the 'ceremonies'. Added to this evangelical fervour was the inculcation of two great principles, the divine right of Presbytery, the almost as sacred institution of the Covenants. At all this the nobility now connived, or secretly encouraged where they did not openly help.

Coincident with the demand, the supply of Presbyterian clergy, partly the handwork of Robert Boyd, began to increase. As a class the lairds were still worthily represented by men such as Boyd himself, Baillie, Douglas, Livingstone, Blair and others. What were their chances of success as the battle for a Presbyterian Scotland began? The great lack of the Presbyterians in the 'Twenties' was a cohesive directorate at the head of affairs. Boyd was a scholar and somewhat of a recluse; Bruce was old and feeble; Dickson had been silenced, and any others were too widely dispersed to hold convenient council. When, in 1637-38, they achieved such a directorate, they became politically irresistible. At present, they were a dispersed command without a G.H.Q. In the Episcopate there existed—in justice to Spottiswood, Sydserf, Maxwell, Forbes—a brilliant one intellectually. But the clerical rank and file were half-hearted and of no high endowment. The Presbyterians, on the other hand, possessed the material of all revolutions—men of intelligence, conviction and zeal. In their work of evangelical and ecclesiastical propaganda, such men were a paramount necessity. Not a few of them, as has been seen, were Boyd's gift to the cause. Their more democratic origin and their native and Calvinist education has already been noted. Logically they found it impossible to separate the Calvinist doctrine from the Presbyterian principle and the Arminian and Episcopal attack on the former only strengthened their assertion of the latter.

These men made full use of their forum—the pulpit—whether

it was in church, chapel, house or heugh. For the propagandist purpose, the spoken discourse, exegetical or hortatory, even the extempore prayer, were far more effective than a liturgy. The Episcopalian lack of preachers, their moderate outlook, their half-hearted obedience to the dictation of Laud and Charles, destroyed them in the battle of pulpits. The instructive exegesis of Scripture, matters of faith and morals, and as the strife became keener, semi-political and even 'treasonable' ideas poured forth from the Presbyterian pulpit. Gradually throughout the Lowlands, the people came to listen with avidity to their doctrine; the only compulsion was their will to hear, for excommunicatory power then rested with the bishop and neither pastor, session nor Presbytery enjoyed their later coercive powers. The sermons of such masters of the pulpit as Dickson, Blair, Rutherfurd, Livingstone show them expressing great doctrines in the simple word and homely analogy suited to the minds of the hearers. Dickson objected to over-elaboration in sermons, because 'the cook should bring no meat to the table, but what the men are to eat' and to make a parade of learning was, 'as if the cook should bring up the spit and raxes to the table, which are fit to be kept in the kitchen to make ready the meat'. Livingstone's instructions on the art of composing sermons might still be practised with profit by most ministers. The Scottish preachers of this age may lack the wit of a Donne or the style of a Taylor, but they converted souls, which is the specific work of a sermon. While in their zeal they may be exuberant on occasion, they never rave in the manner of the later saints of the Covenant. Their sermons were as often exegetical and experiential as theological and polemic, though to neither of the latter sort were they strangers. By their efforts, the people of Scotland from Wigtown to Fife were won to Presbyterianism before 1638, and not terrorised into it afterwards as some historians aver.

A custom grew up, whereby some of the abler ministers would preach in other parishes at Communion seasons or such times as markets when people were wont to gather. Blair, Rutherfurd, Livingstone and Dickson seem to have been in great demand.

The flame of Presbyterianism was kept constantly lit at its fiercest torches. After the Stewarton revival, the value of such meetings impressed itself on the Presbyterians and the practice established itself firmly.

The unwillingness of the bishops to 'place' young men of Presbyterian leanings gave rise to a great deal of itinerant preaching. Blair was charged with it before the Council. Men like Livingstone and Gillespie, unable to find a charge, moved here and there, settling for a little as chaplain under the protection of a Presbyterian baron or laird, and, supported by him, alienating his tenants from the Episcopal cause. Thus instead of being localised where a resident bishop might have controlled them, they were dispersed and more easily spread the infection. Since they moved quickly from jurisdiction to jurisdiction, it was difficult for a non-resident bishop to deal with the matter. These men addressed themselves to groups of the 'well-affected' in each parish, organised and formed even more of them from the leading men in each, thus creating local nuclei of Presbyterian thought and politics. So important did such meetings become that Rutherfurd wrote a treatise, now lost, on their use.

Nor were the Presbyterians unaware of the importance of 'key positions', such as the kirk of the county town, or that situated on a 'main thoroughfare'. The letters to Rutherfurd from what directing body existed in Edinburgh, asking him to get a sound man planted in Kirkcudbright, is an instance of this, and a hundred similar little intrigues were occupying the attention of both sides. The years 1625-39 witnessed a ceaseless juggling for such positions. Moreover, one great necessity of a party conflict the Presbyterians possessed, a definite programme or 'platform'. They had evolved a native system of doctrine and discipline from France and Geneva. They knew unanimously what they wanted and how they wanted it. The Bishops may have known Charles's 'wants' but most of them doubted the wisdom of them, and were at a loss to procure the fulfilment of his wishes. They were themselves also divided doctrinally on the Arminian question. The technique of the controversial pamphlet developed in France. Episcopal control prevented the Presbyterians using the press to a great extent in the early years of the controversy, but the work of Rutherfurd in his early years shows that written 'papers' were constantly circulating surreptitiously. As Charles's power decreased, pamphlets began to circulate more freely. Baillie in 1637 mentions 'the scandalous pamphlets that come daily new from England add oil to the flames'. The Scots soon showed they needed little incentive to the task of controversial pamphleteering.

But we must not forget that those men who were such zealous Presbyterians, were, first of all, great evangelists. An evangelical faith in the real and not the formal sense of the word, took hold of the heart of the Scottish peasant and burgher. The 'Stewarton sickness' has been referred to. It was an evangelical revival in the district around Irvine and Ayr which lasted in intensity during the ministry of David Dickson, in Irvine, especially between the years 1625 and 1630. There were the religiously weak-minded among the converts. There were men of John Brown's kind also. Robert Boyd blessed God for the work and Boyd would give no blessing to anything dubious or spurious. Crowds flooded to sermon, sacrament and private meeting. In Shotts parish also, Livingstone found the same responsive atmosphere. Scotland was not merely being Presbyterianised, she was being thoroughly evangelised and it was being done by Presbyterians. Stewarton and Shotts are but two names. In other places the work went on with quiet but sure success; the success which made it impossible for Laud to force a more formal creed on an awakened Scotland. The man who gave Scotland many of these evangelists was Robert Boyd of Trochrigg.

To me, one of the most attractive of our Reformers has always been Robert Boyd, ever since I read Wodrow's well documented *Life of Robert Boyd*. He along with Bruce was chief in making the men of the 'Second Reformation'. The men whom he taught in Glasgow were to evangelise Scotland. The reserved, cultured, fastidious Professor of Divinity had an influence on his students second to none, except perhaps Melville, and I am inclined to place them equal in this respect. In character they were not unlike except that Boyd lacked Melville's vehemence, but could make up for it, when roused, by the acidity of his tongue. His ancestry was only less illustrious than Bruce's. He was descended from Robert Boyd, Chamberlain to James II, whose son Thomas, Earl of Arran, had such a meteoric rise and fall. The Trochrigg family were descended from the second son, Alexander. Boyd's father was James Boyd of Trochrigg, Bishop of Glasgow, who died in 1581. His mother was Margaret Chalmers of Gaitgirth, a member of the oldest and staunchest Protestant household in Ayrshire, for a Chalmers had been chief among the Ayrshire Lollards. As Boyd was born in 1578 and his father died in 1581, the predominant influence on his early life was the resolute Protestantism of his mother. His intellectual gifts were certainly those of the house of Boyd. He had as cousin that strange figure, Mark Alexander Boyd, eccentric and scholar. As a young man, this cousin was educated by Boyd's father. He was one of the 'bangsters' who early troubled Melville at Glasgow, and leaving there pursued a course as a swashbuckling duellist and gambler in Paris. He then took to his studies seriously and became a competent classicist. He fought for France against the German Princes, studied law, wrote on jurisprudence and took part in a political rising in Toulouse and was imprisoned. Subsequently freed, he varied his occupations between jurist and professional soldier. Returning home, he died at forty in 1601. The gift of tongues ran in the family. Mark Alexander could dictate in three different tongues at once. Notes on Pliny, a translation of Caesar's Commentaries into Greek, Latin poetry and a French political treatise all flowed from his pen. His cousin Robert showed all his intellectual qualities and tastes except that of riotous living. Other cousins, all sharing the talents of the Boyds, were Zachary Boyd, minister and poet, and Andrew Boyd, Bishop of Argyll.

As Robert Boyd never seems in any great straits, he must have inherited some of the Boyd fortunes which escaped seizure in James III's reign or perhaps had been replenished at the Reformation. He was educated at the Grammar School of Ayr and proceeded to Edinburgh University where he was laureated M.A. in

c

1594 and subsequently studied divinity under Rollock. Everywhere he speaks of Rollock with the highest respect, 'incomparable', 'immemorable' are only two of the epithets applied to him. As a teacher, Rollock made an indelible impression on Boyd. There is no record of a sudden 'conversion'. Boyd grew up with a mother firmly attached to Reformation doctrine and had the Church before him as a career from the very beginning. But in the family, the unfortunate experiences of his father as Bishop of Glasgow were still remembered. In trouble with the nobles, in trouble with the Assembly, in trouble with the Regent, in trouble with the ministers whom he nominally supervised, James Boyd had no easy life and died young. A bishop in the age of Morton was more to be pitied than blamed. James Boyd tried to do his work as well as he was able or as circumstances allowed. Robert had no liking for the bishop's place. In Rollock, he saw his own field of service, a teacher of teachers, and he set himself from his early days to equip himself for the task. None ever equipped himself better.

In 1597, the year after James had broken Melville's power, using the anti-Catholic riots as his fulcrum, Boyd set out for France. For a year and a half, he sojourned with Rivet at Tours, teaching in a school founded by the Duc de Tremouille. He quickly learned and mastered the French language, so that he was said to be able to preach better in it than in his native tongue. His name and fame as a scholar quickly procured him a call to be Professor of Philosophy and Polite Learning at Montauban. There is an idea, fostered by some Scots historians, that the Reformers were rude rhetorical agitators and little else. Boyd's career and that of his cousins alone would dispel this idea. The universities of Protestant France were filled with Scots professors —some of them, like John Cameron, with a continental reputation, Robert Weems, Patrick Ramsay, Gilbert Burnett, William Craig, the great Cameron and others held teaching posts in the French Colleges and the Scottish Church owes a great deal of its shape and form to this living contact with the Huguenot Church. Boyd's election as Professor of Philosophy and Polite Learning shows the esteem in which his abilities were held and apart from his Theology, his other publications are volumes of Latin verse which show him as practised as any of his age in that art. He was not the man to teach others without knowing his job by personal experience. In 1604, he left Montauban to become pastor to the Protestant Church in Verteul, where he remained for three years. He was then elected Professor of Philosophy in Saumur in 1607. By 1608, we find that he is Professor of Divinity. There he began his life-long study of Ephesians, lecturing upon that book because he held that the Apostle had in it 'comprised all the chief heads of Divinity'. He happily married a French lady of good family of the house of Malivern. His salary was 600 pieces of gold, a fair sum for these times, and he was enabled to travel as occasion sometimes offered, home to Scotland, always journeying through the good publishing centres. We find him in Frankfurt, Nuremberg, Strasburg, Ratisbon, Heidelberg, Antwerp and London, visiting the booksellers' shops and probably spending much of his salary on the books he loved. He enjoyed his work lecturing. He was a great disciplinarian and believed in the inculcation of good manners. The Boyds, ambitious as the Earl of Arran, or soldiers of fortune like Mark Alexander, his cousin, had all been courtly gentlemen. Of Thomas, Earl of Arran, it was said by an English contemporary, 'He was the most courteous, gentlest, wisest, kindest, most companionable, most bounteous knight.' Unruly conduct and bad manners were anathema to Boyd. He refused to have anything to do with the physical correction of pupils—still needed in the universities—because he believed disciplined conduct to be a thing of the mind. The Professor of Polite Learning gave many a severe lecture to his pupils on the duties of gentlemanly conduct and when he came to Glasgow he was often sorely tried by the behaviour of his students.

He was happy in his work in France, but being a Scotsman, he looked with unhappy eyes on the way affairs were progressing in Scotland and on one occasion he wrote to Bruce, 'I could wish that I had been profitable to my own country and to the Kirk of God within the land.' In 1615, he was finally persuaded to come home to be Principal of Glasgow University. The King undertook to bear the expenses of his travelling—an undertaking Boyd had some difficulty later in having fulfilled. Boyd accepted the appointment with certain reservations, one being that he be not called to exercise physical discipline on any student and another being that he should not be asked to eat with them at the common table. He was a martyr to stomach trouble and the cooking was no doubt crude. Evidently the table manners of the Glasgow students were not all that could be desired either. Boyd had, with the courtliness, some of the fastidiousness of his house. From his own account and that of his contemporaries, we read that his wines, his meat, the horses he used, were all of the best. He had a great fondness for Greek wine and Greek learning. He spent £100 a year on books. Though he did not dine with the students he kept a hospitable table where the worthy student was always welcome and afterwards, when the covers were drawn, he and the favoured students would sit and sing roundels together. The airs of Byrd and of Purcell and of Palestrina softened the grimness of religious controversy. Illness had lined his features, but Livingstone could write, 'Although he was a man of sour-like disposition and carriage, I always found him so kind and familiar as made me wonder.'

He was Principal at Glasgow University from 1615 to 1622. In that short time he turned out the men who were to make the 'Second Reformation'—David Dickson, Robert Blair, Livingstone, Hugh McKail and many others. He had his failures. He found Glasgow ruder and cruder than Saumur. His students' manners worried him, their conduct annoyed him, so that we find him writing, 'This loathsome and to me hateful oversight of a school.' Whatever he may have felt, the job was thoroughly done and he spared no pains either in teaching or in administering the affairs of the College. But Boyd speedily came into conflict with the authorities over the Perth Articles. As minister in Govan, he celebrated the Communion without kneeling. His attitude was, that changes could be imposed on the Church only by a free Assembly, and he refused to accept the changes until the whole

Kirk of the Kingdom, 'freely and willingly, uncompelledly, resolvedly and peaceably receive them with full contentment and approbation'. These were not sentiments to please James and his Bishops and Boyd's stay in Glasgow was foredoomed. Always in Boyd we find this insistence on freedom of the individual to choose his faith. He writes, 'I had rather with the bird have freedom and his commodity than be pent up in a cage and have meat and better cheer laid to my hand.' He could be bribed to no subservience. As the years passed and his contact with Bruce became more frequent, he became more outspoken in utterance till finally he was dismissed from his post. Edinburgh sought to profit by Glasgow's loss. In October 1622, the Town Council appointed him Principal of that College, but in his letter of acceptance he made clear his position. 'I remember I am enrolled in His school to fight out His battles even to that full and final victory, never to give up until He has sounded the retreat.' But James had not outed him from Glasgow to place him in the capital city, so orders went forth to the magistrates to put Boyd out unless he conformed. This he refused to do, so in January 1623 he left Edinburgh for his estate of Trochrigg. John Cameron, more agreeable to a King's command, had become Principal of Glasgow University but found it less to his liking than Boyd and left in 1624, after a brief stay of two years. Attempts were made to bring Boyd back. A conforming formula was proposed, but as in Bruce's case also, it was not enough. He never went back but passed his remaining years as Minister at Paisley, harried and worried by the family of Abercorn. He died at the early age of forty-nine years at Trochrigg, in 1627.

Boyd was perhaps the greatest scholar the Church of Scotland ever possessed. He had all the Boyd gift of tongues. It was said, 'He was more eloquent in French than he was in his mother tongue, more eloquent in Latin than in French, and more eloquent in Greek than in Latin.' His Greek quotations were all from the original without reference and accurate, except on occasion when he would read a somewhat large quotation from Chrysostom. When the lack of culture in seventeenth-century Scotland is deplored, we may remember Boyd, Greek scholar and Latin versifier. He was never a fanatic. Till the Bishops began their insistence on the Perth Articles, he had meddled little with them. 'A man of extensive charity and could bear with such as were of different sentiments from him and very much honour them for other good qualifications', writes his biographer. He was a deeply religious man, because he had been brought up thus. He had ample means but, 'considering the great salvation purchased him by Jesus Christ, he had resolved to spend himself to the uttermost, giving all diligence to glorify that Lord, who so loved him'. He never attended an Assembly and from the first resisted the Perth Articles (Kneeling at Communion, Private Baptism, Private Administration of the Sacrament, Episcopal Ordination and Celebration of Holy Days) as being Romanist. He had lived among Romanists and feared any kindred practice. He left an indelible impression on the minds of his students, who, though they lacked his good taste, held fast to his principles. Blair, Dickson, Livingstone, McKail and Baillie cannot speak too highly of him. Blair said, 'I profited little by others but he was sent of God to me.' Rutherfurd knew and loved him. Baillie who had some of his moderation but little of his greatness of soul, edited his works. He left behind some little-known Latin verse and the great commentary on Ephesians. But he left something more important. He left the men who were to save the free soul of Scotland.

CHAPTER III

THE COVENANTS

THE PERIOD between 1633 and 1643 has been traversed by the pen of so many historians that as far as the development of the political situation is concerned, little that is new can be added here. Two elements dominated and decided the fate of the nation: a preaching Kirk and a protesting and spendthrift nobility. Without the work of the Presbyterian ministers such as Rutherfurd, Dickson, Blair, Livingstone and many lesser men between 1625 and 1638, resistance to Charles might have been much less religious and national, much more political and feudal. Without the support of baron and laird, the Presbyterian would have found his task in the country one of extreme difficulty. The landed classes controlled the ministry of the Church through their patronage, and in the appointment of Rutherfurd and men like him, we have seen them using it as a political weapon to break the power of the Bishops. Scotland swung over to the Presbyterian faith decisively between the Act of Revocation and the Covenant. The establishment of Presbyterianism, therefore, owed something to the political needs of the feudal party but as a creed it was so preached and inculcated by an able and zealous clergy that when the nobles sought later to temper its nature, they failed, and when later still they sought to abolish it, they brought years of suffering and blood on Scotland, and, in the end, again failed. At the present moment, they were paying the piper—as little as possible, of course—but after 1638, for twenty years, the Kirk was to call the tune.

Every act of Charles subsequent to 1627 had driven the two parties into closer alliance. He used all his father's political artifice with none of his father's political cunning. In Scottish affairs James VI had shown much practical wisdom and many good intentions. Charles was quite prepared to treat the land of his birth as a mere province, and nationalist indignation as well as national religion played a part in rousing all classes against him. By an astute arrangement, James had gained control of the Lords of the Articles through an Act of 1609. The nobles chose eight bishops, the bishops chose eight nobles and the sixteen chose eight from the Commissioners for Barons and Burghs. As the bishops were King's men, and chose similarly minded peers, the Lords of the Articles were subserviently Royalist. This Committee drew up all the Acts of Parliament and the Estates merely met again at the end of the session to sanction the bills which it presented. In 1633, on his visit to Scotland, Charles had all his ecclesiastical legislation sanctioned by the Estates. He mulcted Scotland for a heavy grant—to be spent elsewhere—and further raised religious hostility by procuring an Act giving him power to determine 'the apparel of kirkmen'. The Estates sought to offer opposition, but Charles overawed the Assembly and was even accused by the Presbyterians of tampering with the votes. He left after making a few new peers but few new friends.

He proceeded politically from bad to worse. The nobles who had opposed him in 1633 had drawn up a 'Supplication' justifying their course of action—a much milder affair than some of the 'Bonds' with which his predecessors had been browbeaten. A copy found its way out of Lord Balmerino's possession into the hands of Archbishop Spottiswood. Charles had Balmerino tried for high treason—he was found guilty by eight votes to seven, but opinion even among his own supporters forced Charles to use the prerogative of mercy. He only succeeded in further acerbating feudal feeling. His next steps were fatal to the existing ecclesiastical regime.

The Confession of Faith and the Book of Common Order still held their place in the doctrine and worship of the Kirk. There was some dissatisfaction with them, as has been seen, but now, the growing dissatisfaction was more towards having the latter 'purified' than towards the more liturgical revision desired by a few of the Bishops. As the reaction to the Perth Articles and the later 'novations' controversy show, a strong anti-liturgist and

Puritan party was growing up in the Presbyterian ranks and it would be ridiculous to believe that the Presbyterians objected to the Book of Common Prayer only because it was an English imposition, which, despite Scottish editing, it was. They detested it as a liturgy and the method of its introduction utterly destroyed any chance of acceptance. The imposition of the new 'Book of Canons' in 1636 followed by that of the 'Book of Common Prayer' in 1637, without reference to a General Assembly or to Parliament, roused the Presbyterian party to revolt. In anticipation of this, Charles set up the Court of High Commission which caused the fires of the opposition to blaze more furiously.

Principal Hugh Watt believes the instigator of the impositions to have been Laud—and Laud's desires for Scotland, 'that veriest devil that is out of hell' can best be found in his private letters to Wentworth and not in what he afterwards wrote when awaiting trial. He also suggests that Laud was initially responsible for the additions to the Prayer Book which made it even more liturgical in character than the English Prayer Book of which it was largely a replica and that it was his intention, if successful in Scotland, to introduce this more mediaevalised liturgy in England.[1] Dr Gordon Donaldson, following Dr Cooper, believes the Prayer Book alterations, as finally adopted, to have been the work, not of Laud but of the Scottish Bishops, particularly Wedderburn, and seeks to show that in the Prayer Book definite concessions were made to Scottish usage; his work on the Prayer Book is a fine piece of textual research which cannot be altogether ignored.[2] Nevertheless to the people the Prayer Book was 'Laud's Liturgy' and to be hated accordingly; nor was their judgement so far wrong.

Charles and Laud had for years wished to impose the English Prayer Book on Scotland and the final drafting of the Scottish model based upon it fell into the hands of Wedderburn who had lived long in England and was a fervent admirer of Laud. It can be said that the alterations to the English version, if he made them,

[1] Scottish Church History Society Records, vol. 8
[2] Dr Gordon Donaldson, *The Making of the Scottish Prayer Book*

do him credit as a liturgist. But the concessions to Scottish usage —and it is difficult to determine what that usage then was and quite easy to regard the concessions as camouflage which, for example, used the Scottish Communion order but introduced a more liturgical and mediaeval prayer content into it—these concessions were negligible compared to the fact that what the Scots were having forced upon them was an English Prayer Book. During the compilation constant reference was made to Laud who approved Wedderburn's alterations and directly or indirectly inspired them, for his mind moved always towards a more liturgical than towards a less liturgical order and he stated himself that he wished the Scottish additions had place in the English Prayer Book. He, as well as his opponents, saw them as closer to his own liturgical pattern and, granted the power, he would most assuredly have introduced them into England. In pre-Covenant years, there is ground for believing that Charles was trying his hand in Scotland before venturing a further assertiveness in England and as far as ecclesiastical affairs were concerned, Laud was always behind him, even complaining to Wentworth that Charles was not going far enough or fast enough with the ungrateful Scots.

To sum up, the Prayer Book was far removed from the Book of Common Order with the explicit condemnation of transubstantiation and similar doctrines contained in the Communion order of the latter. Presbyterian opinion was resolutely hardening against anything liturgical. To the simple minded the proposed Communion service seemed almost the Mass itself, and, to the more Puritan, it was, with its more liturgical order for the administration of the Lord's Supper, a definite step on the road back to Roman practice. In any case, whether it was only an attempt to Anglicise Scottish practice with as little concession as possible, or whether it was an attempt to 'fly a kite' by introducing a more mediaevalised Prayer Book into Scotland before doing so in England, or whether it was an attempt at the first, with the second a half-formed intention lurking at the back of Laud's mind, the attempt failed in Scotland. That failure encouraged Parliamentary opposition within England which, aided by the Scottish military exploits, contrived the downfall of both Laud and Charles. Two things particularly roused the Scottish temper: the rendition to the King in the Book of Canons of power to determine every detail of ecclesiastical law, discipline and worship, and the 'Romanising' nature of the Prayer Book. As Dr Watt has pointed out, the 'Sacrament' had become the central ordinance of Scottish religious life. Also, as had been seen, the past decade had witnessed the Communion seasons as great well-springs of religious life and conversion through powerful evangelical preaching. To howl Mass in the 'lugs' of the hearers on such an occasion was to them intolerable sacrilege. A break was coming—would have come between Charles and his people without this final insult—for insult it was—flouting every class of his people, Kirk, Estates and Commonality; the opinions, the wishes, the interests, the feelings of none were consulted, but it might not have been so final and decisive but for this mad gamble. Whatever else the Scotsman's religion was, it was anti-Romish; John Knox had inculcated in him, once and for all, hatred of 'Popish practices'. The Thirty Years' War was most bloodily before him and tales of Romish atrocities lost nothing in the telling in an age when they ran from mouth to mouth. He could not be expected to discriminate, as some of his descendants, between the nice distinctions of mediaevalism and Romanism. He saw the apparent forcible intrusion of practices which he believed to be akin to those which his fathers had cast out and he rose in arms against it.

Petition after petition was addressed to the Privy Council against the Liturgy. 'Jenny Geddes' flung her stool in July 1637. The Council temporised by suspending the reading of the Prayer Book till the King's wishes were known. Charles sent back word peremptorily ordering the establishment of the Liturgy. The nobles and lairds, twenty-four of the former, two to three hundred of the latter, drew up, signed and presented the 'National Petition' to the Council demanding the withdrawal of the Service Book and the removal of the Bishops from the Council. In the number of the lairds' signatures, we see how well the parish propagandist and evangelist had done his work; that of Rutherfurd, the greatest of them all, has been noted in relation to this very petition. Further rioting followed. The 'Tables' were formed of four representatives from each of the four orders, nobles, lairds, burghers and ministers and by them a 'Supplication' was again drawn up and presented to the Council. Evasion and equivocation failed that sorely harassed body and they again promised to lay the matter before the King. Charles's reply was an inane proclamation ordering the petitioners to disperse. The 'Tables' replied with the 'National Covenant', ably drafted by Henderson, Hope, and Wariston, based on the negative 'Confession of Faith', drawn up for James VI in 1581. As a condemnation of Romish practices, few could scruple to sign it or the final oath of defence in support of the Crown and true religion. It was a truly national protest, for since the War of Independence all classes had never been so united in a common purpose. There was, of course, some boycott and compulsion in the signing and the other side might complain but had to recollect Charles's conduct in the Parliament of 1633. Aberdeen which had enjoyed teachers and pastors of learning and character alone remained recalcitrant, to be coerced into covenanting by the warrior who later looted her for abiding by the Covenants.

Bit by bit Charles was forced to give way. Book of Canons and Liturgy were withdrawn and a General Assembly called which met at Glasgow in November 1638, with Henderson as Moderator and Wariston as clerk. The Assembly disregarded Hamilton's formal dissolution; Bishops, Canons, Liturgy, Articles of Perth and Court of High Commission were all swept away. Charles resorted to arms, and the fiasco of the First Bishops' War ending in the Pacification of Berwick ensued.

Tension for the moment eased, and an Assembly which had royal sanction was called. To make assurance doubly sure, it sanctioned all the acts of the preceding Assembly and procured an Act in Council imposing the subscription of the Covenant on the whole nation. Hamilton in the 1638 Assembly would give the King's imprimatur to nothing; Traquair, the present Commissioner, was prepared to give it to everything, while seeking at the same time to subvert, by all means in his power, everything to which he assented. Hitherto none of the nobles in the Covenanting party had been outstanding as leaders. Their unity, rather than their leadership, had procured their ends. From 1639 onwards the Earl, subsequent Marquis, of Argyll began to dominate their Councils till their disruption into two parties at the Engagement. Largely through his working, Parliamentary as well as Church reform was extorted from Charles in the next few years.

In 1640 Charles again tried armed coercion, to be ingloriously driven back from the borders of the Northern Kingdom. The Scots occupied Newcastle and stayed there for a year, an unfortunate year for Charles. The Scots in the north gained the abolition of Episcopacy and the legislation of their Covenant and its imposition. Their Commissioners in England saw the fall of Laud, the doom of Strafford, the abolition of the Star Chamber, Court of High Commission and Council of the North; they returned to Scotland, having established friendly contacts with the English Parliament whom the Scottish rising had so timeously helped in its struggle for freedom, and having drawn from the English pockets the sum of £200,000 for army expenses.

When Charles made concessions, they were fatally too little and too late. It now seemed to him politic to win back the nation he had flouted. He had no wish to see the alliance between the militant Scots and the recalcitrant Parliament further strengthened. He came to Scotland determined to please. His autocratic temper was sorely tried. Concession after concession was wrung from him; Parliament was 'democratised' into a free debating Assembly and the appointment of Crown officials and the judges was taken out of his hands and placed in theirs. He succeeded in detaching the discontented Montrose from the main body of the Covenanting party. Montrose's party engaged in an obscure plot to overthrow Argyll by kidnapping him, along with Hamilton who had now entered into political collaboration with Argyll. The plotters even purposed assassination. The 'Incident', as it was called, was ill timed. It showed an utter lack of political capacity in the participants. Charles protested with truth that he had no hand in the business. Montrose was under detention for his share in the 'Cumbernauld Bond'—an anti-Argyll version of the old feudal practice—and his part in the whole affair is obscure. Argyll was astute enough to manage the affair, and possibly to magnify it, so that his power and prestige, on his return to Edinburgh from Kinneil House, whither he and Hamilton had fled for 'safety', was greater than ever. Much has been written about this affair. The truth seems to be that Argyll adroitly used an abortive and gauche attempt of his opponents at the old feudal snatch-and-grab raid to make sound political capital for his party. In the midst of all this the news of the Irish Rebellion and the Ulster Massacres broke upon Scotland. The Scottish hatred for Rome became a bloodthirsty fury directed against Irish Papists. When Charles treated with these same Papists he lost all hope of keeping Scotland either neutral or at his side. Meanwhile he hurriedly flung an earldom to Leslie and a marquisate to Argyll and as hurriedly left the Kingdom. When Charles left, Montrose and his company were let out.

On 22nd August 1642 civil war broke out in England. Both sides sought Scottish help. It was superlatively valuable in the opening gambit. Had Charles received the Scottish help instead of Parliament, he might have won the war by decisive victories at the beginning. Now, more than anything he had done to them by bishops, Ulster lay, a bloody cloud, between him and his people, as the *Lex Rex* reveals. Ulster more than Laud brought Scotland in on the Parliament side. Argyll again used the other side's mistakes. Scotland had beaten Charles twice. Scotsmen could and did treat him rudely, but in the majority of them there existed a natural and perverse resentment against any other nation doing so to a man they still accounted a Scotsman. Such a resentment played havoc with political parties and theories after his execution. Moderate Covenanters now supported the King. The Privy Council by eleven votes to nine decided that the King's communication and appeal to his people for help alone should be read and published. Six weeks or so later, the Commission of Assembly and the Conservators of the peace—a sort of projection of the Tables with more legal sanction—petitioned the Council to publish the message of the English Parliament. The Council in spite of the 'Cross Petition' against such publication had to yield in the face of the strong opposition and not only publish Parliament's communication, but assert that they had published Charles's merely for informatory purposes. In July, the Earl of Antrim was caught with papers revealing that Charles was dealing with the Irish rebels for forces to invade both Scotland and England. Even Andrew Lang cannot explain away this fact though the perturbation it aroused is equated with the 'fearful joy children do find in ghost stories'. One wonders what sort of banshee his seventeenth-century ancestors found Colkitto's ruffians. Argyll revealed Charles's dealings and his cause was doomed in Scotland, doomed all the more when Montrose led Irish caterans to the sack. Only by his death did he win back most of the Scottish swords for his son. As the Liturgy precipitated the National Covenant, so the 'Irish Cessation', as it was called, brought the Solemn League and Covenant into being. The opening para-graph referring to 'the treacherous and bloody plots, conspiracies, attempts and practices of the enemies of God against the true religion and professors thereof in all places especially in these three Kingdoms' is ample evidence of the common fear that cemented the nation. Unity of religion, extirpation of Popery and Prelacy, preservation of Parliamentary privilege, were the objects of the League to be effected by a military alliance. The Scottish Church visualised a Presbyterian England and would have no less as the price of Scottish aid. The English Commissioners kept their thoughts, very closely, to themselves as under the pressure of political necessity they signed for their Parliament this bargain with the Convention of Estates and the General Assembly.

In the following chapters of biography the political story of the Covenant is more intimately told. In the lives and careers of Gillespie and Rutherfurd especially, so closely connected with succeeding affairs and policies, the whole complex issues of the period may be studied. Henderson, the politician and statesman, Gillespie, the propagandist, Rutherfurd the apologist, are the great trio of the Presbyterian cause. They worked best when they worked together and Henderson's death left the other two without the restraining influence they often needed. They were all great men in a great day. If I have, after reading, seemed a little hard on Gillespie, it is only because I saw him between the statesmanship of Henderson and the selflessness of Rutherfurd. He had his own quality of greatness in his unfaltering spirit.

CHAPTER IV

ALEXANDER HENDERSON

ALEXANDER HENDERSON crossed our vision in the dim light of Forgan Kirk when Robert Bruce won him over to the Presbyterian cause. For such a public figure, little is known of his private life. Before the Covenant, he was a little-known country minister passed over by the Episcopate, whose cause he had left. When he came into power, his life was all public, and what he then did was far more important than what he had been. As he never married, and had few relatives, there was little intimate correspondence left to be cherished by proud descendants, and in his later years he had little time for letter-writing of a private nature. He was born in the parish of Creich. His father was probably a feuar in the village of Luthrie but beyond that nothing definite is known, though he may have been related to the Hendersons of Fordel, as he was laid in the burying ground of that family in Greyfriars Churchyard. St. Andrews was conveniently near, so thither he went at the age of sixteen years in 1599, and in 1603 took his degree of M.A., thereafter following the usual practice of an outstanding student and becoming a regent or teacher of philosophy. He was all his life to be keenly interested in education, but from his whimsical description of himself as a pedagogue who read logic and rhetoric to his scholars, it would appear that personally the work of a professor did not appeal to him and it is significant that in the thirty years, or more, that elapsed between his graduation and his rise to political power, no work of any theological or ecclesiastical importance came from his pen. Gillespie, who enjoyed less than half his years, produced four major works and numerous pamphlets. Rutherfurd produced three times as much as Gillespie. Henderson drafted treaties, explained them in pamphlets, but has given us only his small treatise on 'The Government and Order of the Church of Scotland' and a small volume of sermons. He remained as regent until 1612 and seems to have enjoyed his academic life. In the early years, as a student, he must have known the Melvilles before their exile, and the seeds sown by them must have been quickened by Bruce on that day in Forgan. The departure of Melville saw the rise of George Gledstanes as Primate of St. Andrews and eventually, through his influence, Henderson was presented to the parish of Leuchars.

Neither the Episcopal party nor the presentation was popular in Leuchars. When Henderson arrived for the induction ceremony, the doors were barred against him and he and his friends had to make their way in by breaking a window. His speech at the Glasgow Assembly of 1638 voiced regret at the way in which he was introduced, but his ill reception seems to have been the start of young Henderson's doubts on the validity of the Episcopal system, for it was Bruce's sermon 'He that entereth not by the door into the sheepfold but climbeth in some other way, the same is a thief and a robber' that struck home to his heart. Bruce's text may have been coincidence, but, coincidence or intent, there was providence behind it all. Henderson underwent a double conversion. He became a converted Christian and a convinced Presbyterian.

His circle of acquaintances changed. Archbishop Gledstanes had gone and Archbishop Spottiswood had taken his place. We find him now, not in the court of the Archbishop, but in company with men like William Scott of Cupar, one of Melville's staunchest upholders who was yet to incur the wrath of the King. He attended the Assembly of 1616 at Aberdeen, where James first aired the substance of the Perth Articles. He took a more prominent part in the Assembly of 1618 at Perth where the famous Articles were passed into practice—Kneeling at Communion, Private Communion in Urgent Cases, Private Baptism in similar Cases, Episcopal Confirmation and the Observance of Holy Days. As a sign of the way things were going, the ordinary ministers were treated with scant respect, being left to stand about, 'as if their part were only to behold', says Calderwood. To forty-five of the beholders the decisions of the Assembly were a retrograde step towards ecclesiastical servitude and eventual Papacy. They recorded their vote against them with no uncertain voice. Scott, Carmichael and Henderson were the leaders of the opposition. This opposition also tried to have Scott and Henderson translated to Edinburgh but, as this was far too obvious a move in the political game, and far too dangerous to allow, Spottiswood took no steps in the matter. He had no desire to risk a King's favour by planting firebrands in Edinburgh.

The Perth Articles began to cause trouble immediately, not as much trouble as Laud's Liturgy was to cause, but they were the steps of a cannier King than Charles I towards a Liturgy. Henderson refused to give Communion as prescribed, and was reported to the Archbishop. He replied that no contempt was intended but that he was not persuaded of the lawfulness of the ceremony ordered. In August, he was cited with Scott and Carmichael to appear before the Court of High Commission and accused with them of writing the book called *The Perth Assembly*. Actually it was written by Calderwood. As nothing could be proved against them, they were dismissed. A conference was held in St. Andrews between the Archbishop and the opposition. Nothing came of the business and actually the Episcopal party was content to let sleeping dogs lie. The Five Articles remained law in the Ecclesiastical Statute Book but were observed or unobserved with little notice taken either way. James was in London with a Parliament of lawyers troubling his peace, so the Bishops went on with a 'ca' canny' policy.

We enter now the silent years of Henderson's life. He occupied himself with the affairs of his parish. Theology as a study does not appear to have interested him so these quiet years saw no *magnum opus* flow from his pen. To issue pamphlets was dangerous, though I do not think the danger would have deterred Henderson. The Episcopal party controlled the press and it was difficult for a country minister to find a publisher. Stirling, Dumbarton and Aberdeen all sought him as a pastor but he either

refused to go or obstructions were put in the way of his translation to any charge of importance. He was in his fifties before
he found his sphere of service. But though quiet in a quiet place,
he was not speechless and from the teaching and preaching of
Henderson and his fellows the opposition to Episcopacy grew
fatefully large.

We have seen how the Presbyterian ministry was evangelising
the land of Scotland. The older school of bishops troubled them
little and James, with all his insistence on Episcopal government,
walked fairly cannily. But the new King chose new servants.
Charles saw his father's plans for Scotland march with leaden feet,
so he made his own and chose his tools. The leniency of Spottiswood and Law was to be superseded by the diligence of Maxwell,
Sydserf, Forbes and Wedderburn. Spottiswood was drawn into
paths for which he had no great love. The Act of Revocation
and the imposition of the Service Book precipitated the crisis in
Scotland. It is with Henderson's part in it that we are concerned.

Henderson was first stirred from passive to active resistance by
Charles's treatment of Lord Balmerino. The latter, one of the
most lovable and fairminded of the Reformers, was put on trial
for treason because a copy of a letter of protest against the Episcopal Acts of Charles's 1633 Parliament was found in his possession.
Even Charles's friends were 'scunnered' at the action. He was
found guilty by a packed jury, by a majority of one only, and
public protest was so great that Charles had to pardon him.
Archbishop Spottiswood's attack on this Fifeshire laird certainly
united all Fife, laird and labourer, in the cause. Now that Scott
of Cupar was dead, Henderson was the natural leader to whom
the party turned, and the country minister of Leuchars became
the leader of the eastern Presbyterians as David Dickson was
leader of the west. Fife, while Henderson lived, was to be out-
done by none in zeal.

On 23rd July, 'Jenny Geddes' flung her stool when the Service
Book was read. Whatever happened, the city was in a state of
riot. The words, 'Daur ye say Mass at my lug?' ascribed to her,
if apocryphal, at least show what Scotland thought, and the Book

was to Scotland a step back towards papal chains. For days the city was in a turmoil and the Privy Council was sorely troubled how to deal with the situation. Guthrie says, in his Memoirs, that there was a plot, hatched by Henderson and Dickson, with the approval of Balmerino and Sir Thomas Hope. Sheriff Orr takes pains to prove that Hope and Henderson were little likely to have anything to do with it. It certainly would have been risky for Hope, the Lord Advocate, to have attempted it. But according to the story the lawyer and the lord did not appear. It was Henderson and Dickson who stirred up the matrons of Edinburgh to riot. I am inclined to think that Dickson and Henderson did meet the matrons of the town and Dickson, his fiery eloquence getting the better of him, stirred them up to opposition. We have to remember that public riot was the people's only way of protest against unpopular legislation, and it took courage to riot. Sheriff Orr forgets that, though the Covenanters ultimately took a legal form of action, the power behind the action was popular revolt. Sore diseases need sore remedies.

But it may have been the association with Dickson—for the two men met to consider a concerted course of action for east and west—that made Henderson see that popular agitation was not enough. He saw Dickson's value as a propagandist, as an evangelist and as an agitator, but he saw he was not the man to plan a systematic legal attack on the hated impositions. It was the realisation of this weakness in Dickson that threw Henderson into alliance with the man who was then the most brilliant young lawyer in Scotland, Archibald Johnston of Wariston. It would have been well for Wariston if he had fulfilled the promise of these early Covenant days. From now on the ordered attack begins. Henderson and Wariston became the guiding minds in the legal fulfilment of a nation's desires. Disorderly riot is superseded by legal petition.

Henderson had by now focused the attention of the Episcopalians on Fife and himself. The Archbishop raised letters of horning against him and two other ministers for refusing to buy the Service Book. Henderson petitioned the Privy Council to suspend the charges. His defence was able. He said he had offered to buy books for information but not for practice and refused to use them on the grounds that they were not warranted by any Act of Parliament or by any Act of a General Assembly and were contrary to the former practice of the Kirk. 'The Kirk of Scotland', he states, 'is an independent Kirk, and her own pastors should be most able to discern and direct what does best seem our measure of Reformation and what may serve most for the good of the people.' Further the new Service Book points 'most natural for the Kirk of Rome, for her hierarchy and doctrine, superstition and idolatry in worship, tyranny in Government and in wickedness every way as anti-Christian as when we came out of her.' The Council ratted on the monarch who had appointed them by interpreting their own Act imposing the Liturgy to mean that ministers were to buy the Service Book and no more; surely one of the most comical decisions ever arrived at by any Council. Charles wrote at once telling them that either he had a very slack Council or very bad subjects. But this very much pestered body was now besieged by petition after petition against the Service Book and could hardly convict two thirds of a nation for treason. George Gillespie, greatly daring, had published his *Dispute against the ancient Popish Ceremonies*, and the whole land was in a ferment. Charles's measures to reduce Edinburgh by removing the Council and Law Courts to Linlithgow only further stirred up the opposition and, as was seen, the Tables were set up, in November 1637, one of the most democratic events in Scotland's history. The Tables were comprised of four noblemen, four burghers, four barons and four ministers, who sat in Parliament House to draft grievances and present them to King and Council. The leading spirits were Henderson, Rothes, Loudon and Wariston, Balmerino and Dickson. Their Petitions were unanswered. Charles finally tried to quash them by Proclamation through the Council—government by edict or ukase. It was against this final issue of the matter that the nation entered into Covenant. While we think of it as a protest against Liturgies and a protest against the destruction of

Presbyterianism, it was also a banding together of the people to resist something there has often been need to resist, government of Scotland from Westminster. Henderson was a great Scotsman as well as a great Presbyterian. When process by ordinary petition was denied them, the only alternative was a band—not the old feudal band in which the barons united to thwart the monarch or murder a rival—but a band in which all the nation would be united in its common defence.

Whose was the original idea of the Covenant? We do not know. The first suggestion of a banding together may have been Loudoun's and Henderson immediately fastened on the idea but suggested that they go much deeper than a mere defensive band. His mind went back to the old anti-Romish Confession of 1581 and 1590 and with Wariston he proceeded to shape it to present needs. It is interesting to note that, not to the lawyer, but to Henderson, it was given to draft the addition pertaining to the modern situation. One thing the years of quiet had done, was to make him a man of cool judgement. By Wednesday 28th February 1638, the Covenant was shaped. As we have seen, the first part is the abjuration of all the old Roman Catholic practices; the second part is a protest against the introduction of anything harking back to them. The legal references are Wariston's, the note of earnest puritanism Henderson's. The Covenanters agree to renounce all the practices lately introduced and oppose any not warranted by the Kirk. They agree to unite in their own defence, not violently. At the end come the great words, 'and because we cannot look for a blessing from God except that with our profession and superscription we join such a life and conversation as becometh Christians who have renewed their Covenant with God: We therefore faithfully promise for ourselves, our followers and all others under us, both in public and in our particular families, and personal carriage to endeavour to keep ourselves within the bounds of Christian liberty and to be good examples to others in all godliness, soberness and righteousness and of every duty we owe to God and man.' This could only be Henderson's. The Covenant was signed in Greyfriars Kirk by the leaders.

Thereafter copies were sent throughout the land and all Scotland pledged herself to revive the church of Knox and Melville. The opposition was negligible. It must be admitted that there was some compulsion here and there. But it was only here and there. Henderson was now the leader of Scotland. Dundee made him a burgess on the ground of 'Distinguished Services to the State'. So busy was he in national affairs that his own kirk fell into a state of disrepair and he had to take legal action against the heritors to have it reconditioned for public worship. But he was not to remain much longer at Leuchars. A place had to be found where his voice could be heard daily by the rulers of the nation. In May 1638 he was elected minister of Greyfriars but in January 1639 he moved to the kirk of Knox and Bruce, being elected by the Town Council, Minister of the High Kirk. From there he could direct more easily the affairs of Kirk and State.

Charles sought to have the Covenant declared treasonable. Even the Crown officials would accept no responsibility for doing so. In June he saw the wisdom of concession and sent the Duke of Hamilton north with a Declaration abolishing the Service Book and discarding the Perth Articles but demanding that his subjects sign the Confession of 1590, i.e. the Confession embodied in the National Covenant disregarding the later additions. He also granted warrant for a General Assembly to be held in Glasgow in November 1638. The Covenanters accepted the concessions but refused to sign the King's Covenant. A Protestation was drawn up. The greater part of it was the work of Henderson, exposing the hollowness of Charles's offers. Charles was incensed. He always was when people doubted his word, even when he was employed in double and triple dealings behind their backs. The Assembly met on 21st November, and Henderson was immediately chosen Moderator. Hamilton made it clear that the King would grant everything but the abolition of bishops and also that he would consent to nothing done in the Assembly while lay elders were a component part. Henderson protested their loyalty but maintained the right of the elders to sit in Assembly. It was the final show-down between the two systems

—bishops or elders? To keep the bishops meant that the royal tyranny always had its agents. To keep the elders meant that the people had a voice in the council of the Church. Our very divisions show that the Presbyterian system has allowed its people to choose their own worship. The Assembly kept its elders. Hamilton ordered it to be dissolved but Henderson gave the reply in words that are immortal in Presbyterian annals, 'All that are here know the reason of the meeting of this Assembly, and albeit we have acknowledged the power of Christian Kings for convening of Assemblies and their power in Assemblies, yet that may not derogate from Christ's right; for He has given divine warrants to convoke Assemblies whether magistrates consent or not. Wherefore, seeing we perceive men to be so zealous in their master's commands, have we not also reason to be zealous toward our Lord and to maintain the rights and privileges of His Kingdom?' Henderson's sermons are sometimes prosy but often his words are loaded with power and dignity. He was a great Protestant. None could protest with more force and dignity and an utter absence of temper. To see this, you have only to compare his protests with the later vitriolic and abusive protests of Gillespie and Wariston. All the innovations of Charles were swept away. Episcopacy was abolished and Presbyterian Church government restored. It was revolution, but, as Sheriff Orr points out, the Scots had no other way to preserve their liberties. If the fate of the Bishops was hard, it was not the fate of Guthrie, of Renwick, of John Brown or of Margaret MacLachlan.

Charles resorted to force of arms. The Bishops' War ensued. Henderson issued an able pamphlet, *Instructions for Defensive Arms*, in which he justified the people's right to defend themselves. It was based on Buchanan's *De Jure Regni*. Its main argument is *salus populi suprema lex*. He dwells on the idea of covenant between king and people developed in the old Conciliar School, now more pertinent than ever. He makes it quite clear that the Scots attempt no revolution against the throne. 'Had our throne been void and our voices sought for the filling of Fergus' chair, we would have died ere any other had sitten on that fatal marble but Charles alone.' At the Pacification of Berwick, Henderson and Charles met. As men, they agreed quite well together ,but Charles took a dislike to Wariston which his son inherited, a dislike which cost Wariston his head. Charles allowed a free General Assembly to ratify the decisions of the former, which was held with the results we have already noted; after further frustrations, again Charles resorted to war, levying subscriptions from English Roman Catholics and seeking to bring over an Irish army. Again he was beaten, and the Scots this time went to London to settle the final terms of peace. It was in London, in 1641, that the idea of a Presbyterian Britain began to seize hold of Henderson's mind.

When they arrived in England, the Scots Commissioners found themselves remarkably welcome, and, as distinguished visitors, remarkably overcharged at the inns. The short months of their stay saw Laud imprisoned, Strafford executed, the Court of High Commission overthrown. St. Antholin's Church was put at the disposal of the ministers and Henderson, Baillie and Gillespie preached solid Presbyterian doctrine to a packed church. The English Parliament was debating the future of the Church of England and Henderson perceived a golden opportunity. The ordinary Englishman, despite abuses in his Church, had no objection to a limited Eposcopacy. In a tract, *The Danger and Unlawfulness of Limited Prelacy*, Henderson sought to destroy this 'illusion'. During his stay in London, more papers on the matter flew from his pen and the fire he kindled burned long after he had left for he directed the mind of the English Puritan to the Presbyterian order as an alternative to Episcopacy. By the time he returned, in 1643, there was a considerable Presbyterian party in England. It is usual to call his conduct of affairs at this time a political mistake, yet there was sound reasoning behind his schemes. A limited Episcopacy had developed into a tyrant's tool in Scotland and Henderson believed that the one way to a common peace between the two nations lay in their possessing a common faith. The English Parliament was not prepared to accept Scottish overtures on Church Union and the Scots returned in 1641 having wrung spiritual and political independence out of Charles by the implementation of the Treaty of Ripon and having made valuable contacts in England for a later date.

Between 1638 and 1643, Henderson spent his time and patience reorganising the affairs of the Kirk. The task of reconciling the conservative and radical Covenanters was no easy one—as we shall see when we come to study Rutherfurd—and Henderson fell out of favour with the extremists. When Charles came to Scotland in 1641, it was hinted that Henderson had been bought because he had accepted the appointment of Dean of the Chapel Royal. Weary of it all, he would have taken a small country parish, but Edinburgh, frightened at the thought of losing him, bought him a house in a good situation in the High School Yards. Scotland was soon to need his leadership. On 28th October came the Irish Rebellion and the brutal massacre of the Protestants in Ulster. Public opinion in Scotland associated Charles's Queen with the happenings and Charles left Scotland never to return.

When the Civil War broke out in England, both Charles and Parliament fished for Scottish help. The latter sent letters to Scotland blaming Papists and Prelatists for depriving England of the great advantages that might have been enjoyed through closer union with the Church of Scotland. At Oxford, in 1642, before the Solemn League and Covenant was signed, Henderson tried to bring Charles to agree to some common scheme of uniformity as a condition of peace and became embroiled with Jeremy Taylor in the endeavour. Charles would have none of it. The Scots finally sided with the Parliament and the determining factor was undoubtedly the Irish Cessation. Charles made peace with the Irish to free his troops for the struggle with Parliament and it was suspected—and rightly—that he meant to use the Irish also. The butcheries of Montrose's Irish troops were never forgotten by the Lowlander and provoked the Scots into savage reprisals. At present, the discovery of Antrim's plot brought the Scots, in self-defence, to the side of the Parliament.

The instrument which brought them in was the Solemn League and Covenant; the condition, the promised reformation of the

English Church. Did Scotland try to force her religion on England? In answering the question let us remember that Henderson believed that the majority of Englishmen wished a change in their ecclesiastical order, and from the sycophantic letters of Parliament, he might well be justified in believing this. He saw in uniformity of faith the way to peace; he welcomed the promised Assembly where the measure of a full uniformity should be discussed, determined and agreed; and he and his fellows set out for Westminster with their hopes high.

The tale of Westminster will be told later. Henderson spoke very little in the debates. His health was now far from good but he was always in demand wherever there was need to frame some proposition in committee. At first he was favourably disposed to the Independent members in the Assembly and wrote a preface for one of Burroughs's books; soon, however, his passion for uniformity drove him into a deep dislike for sectarianism, as he found England full of 'monsters of opinions' because of its lack of good Church government. He and Loudoun intrigued, with little success, to have Cromwell impeached as an 'incendiary'. His one great speech in the Assembly was when he trounced Nye who had denounced Presbyterianism as being incompatible with the civil state. He was a diplomatist rather than a dialectician. At Uxbridge, in 1645, he again sought to bring Charles to terms which, as they involved the establishment of Presbyterianism in England, were refused by the King. He granted the terms to three other Scotsmen when it was too late; at present the news of Inverlochy encouraged his resistance. By May 1646 he was writing to the Queen to invite the Pope and other Roman Catholics to help him on promise of liberty of conscience for the Roman Catholics, when he already had surrendered to the Scots.

Henderson spent his dying days reasoning with Charles. The whole issue at stake was Presbyterianism or Episcopacy and the debate was carried on with dignity between the two men. Henderson argued from the point of view of a converted Episcopalian trying to show Charles how he had come to regret that ecclesiastical system. Neither controversialist gave way. In these last reasonings of Henderson there is none of the vehemence of a Knox, none of the vitriol of a Gillespie, only sadness. 'Mr Henderson is dying most of heartbreak at Newcastle', wrote Baillie. He returned home by sea to die in his own house on 19th August 1646 and was buried in Greyfriars Churchyard.

Alexander Henderson was a great Scotsman. His worst foes could find no meanness in his nature. His outstanding political virtue was his patience; there was, in this age of violence, a calm deliberation about all his actions. When later Wariston was left to go his way without Henderson's restraining hand, the results were temporarily disastrous for the Kirk. It is easy to criticise his desire for religious uniformity. It was rooted in his love of peace. Today the erroneous belief that uniformity of political faith can bring peace and security also persists. Unity without uniformity is a sounder political and ecclesiastical situation than uniformity without unity but the present generation is no wiser than the seventeenth century in this respect. Henderson was defeated by the fact that he could not destroy the individuality of the English nation. England chose her own religious way despite Henderson, even despite Cromwell, though not entirely uninfluenced by them. Henderson reconciled the differing parties in Scotland long enough to establish her Kirk for good. Perhaps he did something for the Church of England, or in England, for in the years of contact there, he helped to foster and strengthen the thorough-going Protestant and Puritan tradition which kept the Anglican Church from moving towards a more Roman doctrine and practice. He was eager to promote every effort to educate his countrymen. He introduced legislation into the General Assembly to have schools established in every parish and to create bursaries to support at college the sons of poor parents who had proved ability. At the same time, regulations as to the granting of degrees were tightened up so that none should take their schooling lightly. As Rector of Edinburgh University, he reorganised and strengthened its administration and founded its library, doing the latter for St. Andrews also.

Henderson's insight saw that his nation could not linger in a half-way house. As long as Scotland's form of Protestantism was uncertain and at the mercy of a monarch's fancy, the danger of Papacy seemed to him an imminent reality. By framing the Covenants, he not only preserved Presbyterianism in Scotland, but perhaps Protestantism in Britain.

CHAPTER V

GEORGE GILLESPIE

GEORGE GILLESPIE was the son of John Gillespie, minister of Kirk-caldy. The father, according to Livingstone, was a 'thundering preacher', but the lightning wit of the son was an inheritance from his maternal grandfather, Patrick Simpson, minister at Stirling from 1590 to 1618. Simpson was a great lover of Greek learning, as were not a few of the Scottish Reformers of the late sixteenth and early seventeenth centuries. An able classicist and the first early church historian of the Church of Scotland, his two short histories were republished in 1624 as the *History of the Church since the Days of Our Lord*. In his later years he mastered Hebrew and took up cosmography, showing all the versatility he transmitted to his grandson. Simpson's wit was quick and re-markably gracious for his age. Of a peace-loving disposition, though opposed to Episcopacy he sought no violent means for its overthrow. 'It is enough', he wrote, 'to have liberty to teach Christ's gospel and to die in God's peace and the King's.' A moderate Evangelical of the finest stamp, he handed down the receptive mind, the talent of tongues and the quickness of wit to his grandson, but not the patient spirit that earnestly strove for peace. The violent and impulsive temperament of George Gillespie must have been the gift of his thundering father. As a child he gave no promise of that early brilliance that was to astonish Assemblies and Parliaments. He was accounted 'dull and softlike' by his mother, whose favourite was the younger and more specious Patrick. The father is reputed to have recognised the latent powers of the elder boy and to have prophesied a great future for him.

He lost his dullness quickly. Born on 27th January 1613, he graduated A.M. in St. Andrews in 1629. In that year he received a bursary from the Presbytery to aid his upkeep at St. Andrews.[1] The session of Kirkcaldy agreed to give 'as much money for his entertainment as Dysart gives', which was 20 merks. He cannot have been anything but an exceptionally brilliant student, yet no regentship fell to him. The reasons are obvious. His extreme youth, for he was precocious in an age of precocious young men, prevented him from being placed in a position of authority. He was the grandson of Simpson, who courteously but firmly had nothing to do with Bishops. 'They could not pervert me,' the old man had said, 'and I could not convert them.' His father held similar views and probably expressed them less courteously, and George Gillespie, more than father or grandfather, recked not what he said, how he said it, or about whom it was said. No teacher's pet or bishop's darling, he had to spend nine years in the wilderness before the Church, for great good and some ill, gave him a high seat in her councils.

The appointment as Presbytery Bursar in 1629 suggests that after his graduation as A.M. he remained to study Divinity. From May 1630 until September 1631 there are sundry references to him in the Kirkcaldy Presbytery records as the bursar of Theology. He thus intended entering the ministry from the very outset of his career. It would be unfair perhaps to accuse the Bishops altogether of deliberately keeping him out of the active ministry of the Church, as a lad of eighteen or nineteen years, however precocious, could hardly have exercised an active pastoral ministry with profit to himself and his hearers. Through Rutherfurd's influence he was appointed by Viscount Kenmure, his domestic chaplain. Rutherfurd was a frequent visitor to the Kenmure residences in Galloway and between the two men there grew up a life-long attachment. Gillespie was to pick Rutherfurd's brains on more than one occasion and present in brilliant debating form the thought and argument he gleaned from that even more copious and teeming mind. To be in Galloway with Samuel Rutherfurd was better than slumbering under Howie in St. Andrews. Rutherfurd was Gillespie's post-graduate university

[1] *The Presbyterie Booke of Kirkcaldie* (Ed. Wm. Stevenson, Kirkcaldy, 1900), p. 8

and he learned avidly from the master Presbyterian scholar of the age. He was happy in his duties in the Kenmure household. Lord Kenmure gave him a death-bed commendation which offers the reader of his *Dying Speeches* a hint that Gillespie was a little more outspoken than a chaplain to a great man was supposed to be. Kenmure's death altered the domestic arrangements of his widow, and Gillespie moved to the household of the great Presbyterian noble of the south-west, the Earl of Cassillis—grandson of the roaster of Commendators. There he remained as domestic chaplain and tutor to the heir, Lord Kennedy, till 1638. Cassillis was a man of some principle who neither truckled to the Kirk in her power nor forsook her ministers when later still she fell on evil days. At once a staunch Presbyterian and staunch Covenanter, he behaved kindly to the enthusiastic young zealot who came to him from Kenmure. He was accustomed to write the sermon for Sunday and have his chaplain examine servants and children on it. Both lord and chaplain had a thirst for edification, and the canny Earl and the witty zealot must have enjoyed these early days before the Earl grew dour and the pastor sour.

While with Cassillis Gillespie made his first incursion into the field of political pamphleteering. In 1637 there appeared in Scotland *A Dispute against the English Popish Ceremonies*. For a time none guessed the author and none suspected the young chaplain of Cassillis. The book was printed in Holland, and it is not impossible that the noble pocket bore some of the cost; all being part and parcel of the plan to destroy Episcopal supremacy. The first able literary attack on Charles's policy, the book was as sensational in the politics of seventeenth century Scotland as the letters of Junius were in the politics of eighteenth-century London. It was almost as pungent. Too large to be called a pamphlet, its object was to stir up opposition to the ceremonies and its art shows, with all its learning, the aggressive style of the pamphleteer. Gillespie is far more lucid and orderly in his presentation of the argument than Rutherfurd; his learning, though not as encyclopaedic, is simple and abundant. He hits hard and goes on hitting with many a trenchant phrase and ironic gibe. In four

E

sections he attacks the necessity, the expediency, the lawfulness and the indifferency of the ceremonies, and gave the first tilt to the mitre that 'Jenny Geddes' was to shake and the Covenant tumble from the head of the Bishops. The Council called in all copies of the work and ordered them to be burned by the hangman. Few were surrendered. The book made Gillespie the penman of the Covenanters. Rutherfurd was to be their scholar, Henderson was to be their statesman, Gillespie their pamphleteer. When he read the book, Robert Baillie could hardly believe it was written by so young a man. The *Dispute* was a little too strong for his stomach, and he wrote, 'If that book be truly of his making, I admire the man though I mislike much of his matter; yea, I think he may prove among the best wits of this isle.'[1] Gillespie took a still further part in the Covenant pamphleteering. In the summer of 1638 there appeared a small pamphlet of two sheets, *Reasons for which the Service Book urged upon Scotland should be refused*. So able a pamphlet was it that Baillie took the writer to be Henderson, but he later discovered that the author was Gillespie.[2] These four pages are the most succinct and pithy presentation of the case against the Service Book that I know. In one phrase he damns all ceremonious liturgies. 'It quenches the Holy Spirit because he gets no employment.'

When the Covenant broke the power of the Bishops one of the first acts of the Presbyterian party was to find a parish for the author of the work that had caused so great an uproar and broke the keys of St. Andrews. The charge of Wemyss in Fife was in the hands of the Town Council of Edinburgh, and Gillespie, on the suit of the Earl of Wemyss, was presented to the charge on 5th January 1638. The presentation and ordination was very carefully managed. The Archbishop ordered Robert Douglas to try Gillespie himself, but as Moderator of the Presbytery, he ignored Spottiswood's request and took the matter to his court. On 11th January the Presbytery appointed a day for the trial sermon, and the text, 2 Thess. 11 and 13. On 18th January he preached and was accepted by the brethren.[3] The month of

[1] R. Baillie, *Letters* i, 90   [2] *Ibid.* i, 90   [3] *Presbyterie Booke*, p. 122

February and the Covenant intervened. All the Presbytery of Kirkcaldy but three signed the Covenant. On Wednesday, 11th April, Wariston received a letter from Gillespie asking him to 'clear the Presbytery of Kirkcaldy of their legal doubts anent the admission of ministers.' The letter was obviously sent, for Gillespie was ordained by the Presbytery on 26th April. The ordination of Gillespie by the Presbytery on the very doorstep of St. Andrews was a calculated act of defiance and practically the first patent act of disavowal of Episcopal ordination. Robert Kerr had been ordained colleague to his father at Prestonpans on 11th April by the Presbytery of Haddington, but this had not the same political significance as the ordination of an already notorious Covenanter against the will of the Archbishop. Ordination by Presbytery became the general rule and the November Assembly destroyed the other alternative altogether.

Little is known of Gillespie's work as a parish minister. He spent too little of his short life in a pastoral charge to gain any great skill in dealing with the sufferings and sorrows of ordinary folk, and we find him writing little about them. Though he was able to give all to a cause, and did give all, he was self-engrossed and somewhat egocentric in many ways—qualities even more obnoxious in his brother Patrick. Wemyss has no minutes now extant concerning Gillespie's ministry. The session records diligently kept by him are lost. Administratively, under Gillespie, Wemyss was a model parish. A Presbytery visitation in May 1640 found ministers, elders and reader all without fault, a happy state of harmony existing among them.[1] The morals of Isobel Dick and Peter McKenzie gave recurrent trouble throughout his short ministry.[2] One poor woman, Janet Durie, was examined for witchcraft by the Session and Presbytery and finally sent for trial.[3] Few escaped condemnation even when the charge was ridiculously tenuous. A surly ruffian had killed the poor woman's pig and been told he would rue it. When he fell sick the usual accusation of witchcraft was brought against her. Fife, especially Burntisland and Dysart, has a bad reputation in witch burnings, and Gillespie

[1] *Presbyterie Booke*, p. 175   [2] *Ibid.*, p. 160 etc.   [3] *Ibid.*, pp. 136, 141

seems as credulous as the rest of his age in this matter. For the rest
he was diligent in his business. He had sixty-three elders and
heritors in Wemyss. He was, I think, a presbytery man more
than a parish man. Along with John Smith he examined Dr
Lamont of Markinch, one of the non-covenanting ministers, who
was subsequently deposed.[1] He preached at various Communions
throughout the Presbytery. When not a Commissioner to the
Assembly, he was usually sent as an assessor to the ministers that
were. Towards the end of his Wemyss ministry, he was delegated
to deal with the Privy Council on the matter of collections for
the Irish refugees. These collections were handed into a central
fund in Edinburgh, but Kirkcaldy Presbytery, through Gillespie,
sought and obtained leave to retain some of the money collected
for the use of refugees within their own bounds.[2] Like other parish
ministers he was canonised when he departed, and Gillespie departed in a halo. His successor, Mr Harry Wilkie, seems to have
been irked by having the name of Gillespie always cast up at him.
In 1657 Mr Wilkie had been rather merry at his brother's wedding
but the Synod found him guiltless of any serious impropriety.
He had a good fling at the Gillespies, Patrick especially, by saying
that 'at least he thanked God he was neither a complyer with
enemies nor yet a pluralist pensioner nor politician'. A very
palpable hit, for Patrick was all of them. In October Gillespie was
presented to the parsonage of Methil by David Lord Elcho, which
became part of the charge until Methil was constituted a *quoad
sacra* in 1839.[3] At the Assembly of 1638 which overthrew the
Episcopacy, Gillespie was one of the preachers; preaching on the
text, 'The King's heart is in the hand of the Lord', he went too
far for the leaders of the party. 'He did encroach too much on
the King's actions', says Baillie.[4] Argyll and Henderson after the
sermon advised the brethren to be careful in what they said about
Authority. Gillespie had the kind of tongue that could win a case
and lose a cause. When the Bishops' War threatened he was soon
to the fore with another pamphlet on defensive war. This, if

---

[1] *Presbyterie Booke*, p. 138   [2] *Ibid.*, p. 206   [3] *Ibid.*, p. 136
[4] R. Baillie, *Letters* i, 146

printed, is not now extant. It was so incautious that Henderson
had to write another paper, *The Instructions*, to be read from the
pulpits to counteract any ill effect that Gillespie's pamphlet might
have in alienating moderate men from the party. Gillespie in fact
was now the able backbencher who has to be taken into the
Cabinet. His colleagues were never sure how to control him.
Once set on, he was not so easily pulled off. He was, as Baillie
says, 'too rash a youth in his determination'.[1] In April 1639 he is
found with the Synod of Fife diligently establishing the Presbyterian regime within its bounds, the first meeting at which the
Bishop did not preside.

In 1641 Gillespie, at the age of twenty-eight years, had become
such a figure in the Church that he was chosen with Blair, Baillie
and Henderson as an Ecclesiastical Commissioner in the matter of
implementing the Treaty of Ripon. There was a certain purpose
in the choice of these men, for Henderson had now set his mind
on the creation of a Presbyterian Britain. Baillie writes 'that it
was thought meet that not only Mr A. Henderson, but also Mr R.
Blair, Mr George Gillespie and I should, all three, for diverse ends,
go to London; Mr Robert Blair to satisfy the minds of many in
England who love the way of New England better than that of
Presbyteries used in our Church; I for the convincing of that
prevalent faction against which I have written; Mr Gillespie for the
crying down of the English ceremonies of which he has written.'[2]
When they arrived in London they assiduously applied themselves
to the task of Presbyterian propaganda; too assiduously for either
Parliament or King. Henderson fell foul of Charles with a little
'quick paper' which he issued. Parliament, who were still toying
with the idea of a primitive Episcopacy on Ussher's model, gave
the Scots the evasive answer that this matter of religious uniformity would be taken into consideration later. The Scots Commissioners were successful in establishing their own freedom and
filling the Scottish Exchequer, and the visit made valuable contacts for a later day. The Scots ministers preached on Sunday and
often on weekdays in St. Antholin's Church to large congrega-

[1] R. Baillie, *Letters* i, 186   [2] *Ibid.* i, 269

tions. They were heard as men who had won freedom and London at least became thoroughly acquainted with Presbyterian doctrine. Contacts were made with leading Puritan divines such as Twisse. Blair wrote an answer to Bishop Hall's *Remonstrance* which has been lost, if ever printed. Henderson wrote his *Government and Order of the Church of Scotland*, the most succinct setting forth of the Scottish system yet written. Gillespie wrote *The Assertion of the Government of the Church of Scotland*, a lucid and orderly exposition and defence of the system outlined by Henderson. Baillie was busy also with the publication of *The Unlawfulness and Danger of Limited Episcopacy*. The Scots were determined that Episcopacy, limited or unlimited, must be torn out of the two Kingdoms. The first part of Gillespie's work is an exposition of the Scottish doctrine of the eldership, and begins with a strong repudiation of the term lay as applied to the elders and the word clergy as applied to the ministers. The second part is as able an exposition of the system of church courts. The four propagandists left the English Puritan with a good deal of material for thought. The Presbyterian ideal was for the first time being placed systematically before him. Hitherto English Presbyterianism, both actually and theoretically, had been formless and ill-defined.

Gillespie returned to Scotland with his reputation greatly enhanced. So much so that the Town Council of Aberdeen appointed him as one of their ministers without asking his consent. Doubtless Aberdeen deemed that so young a man would be flattered by being presented to a charge in the leading city of the north-east. Gillespie, who never placed a low value on himself, had other thoughts. The Assembly of 1641 refused to translate him, giving the reason that they wished to keep him near St. Andrews. But Gillespie had his eyes on Edinburgh. Andrew Cant had also been appointed to Aberdeen and had written to Gillespie on the matter. Cant too would have liked Edinburgh, and in his correspondence with Aberdeen Council and with Gillespie is somewhat acidulous. But Gillespie would not be manoeuvred into going where he had no desire. Making Aberdeen's high-handed appointment of him without approach his excuse, he wrote with dry irony, 'Besides if I must transport at all with you, I will hearken to any other sooner nor to Aberdeen. They are indeed in need of a better minister and you are worthy of a better colleague than I am; but I wish both ye and they without more trouble set your mind upon another, for if I be not very far mistaken ye will be disappointed of me.'[1] This modesty was no obstacle to his becoming minister of Greyfriars, Edinburgh, the following year. Nor did it prevent him becoming engaged in an intrigue with his cousin by marriage, the notorious Will Murray, to have his brother Patrick installed as minister in Glasgow Cathedral. A minority of the Town Council supported Patrick's presentation, but the majority opposed on the grounds of his youthfulness. Gillespie, through Will Murray, had got the King, who had the patronage, to present Patrick to the Cathedral. Opposition in the Council and Presbytery was so strong that another was eventually appointed.[2] This same connection with the Murray family was to save Patrick's neck when James Guthrie, a finer man, was hanged. There was a good deal of the careerist in both Gillespies, and Baillie hints that when George was translated to Edinburgh in 1642, his apparent reluctance at the Assembly was histrionic if not indeed tendentious.[3] Balfour records that in September 1641, during Charles's last visit to Scotland, Gillespie, still minister at Wemyss, preached before him in the Abbey Church from the fifth chapter of Corinthians. The text is not given—most likely verse 15, 'Purge out the old leaven.' He never held his hand whether the advantage was fair or unfair. In October 1641 Commissioners from the Presbytery at Edinburgh sought to have Gillespie translated to Greyfriars, but as the Synod of Fife had already consented to his translation to St. Andrews, the matter was remitted to a Committee of Assembly meeting in November, and apparently by them to the Assembly which met in August 1642, and translated Gillespie to Greyfriars. He went, selling his manse to Mr Harry Wilkie, his successor, for 500 merks. Greyfriars had little of him as a pastor and not much

---

[1] Spalding, *Memorials* ii, 484-485
[2] Baillie, *Letters* ii, 5   [3] *Ibid*. ii, 47

as a preacher for he was moved to the High Kirk on his return from London in 1647.

In the years between his ordination and his sojourn in England, from which he returned with an English accent, Gillespie identified himself with the ultra-Puritan party in the Church during the 'Novations' controversy. The extremists of the south-west objected to the use of the Lord's Prayer and the Gloria Patri in public worship, also the minister bowing in the pulpit in private prayer before the service. They also encouraged the use of the Conventicles or private meetings for private edification. The bulk of the Presbyterian party favoured the old usages also, since the occasion for private meetings—among Presbyterians at least —had passed, and since these meetings sometimes deteriorated into a prayer slanging of an unliked minister, there was a general feeling that they should be discontinued. The controversy dragged on for about three years with Gillespie and Rutherfurd giving but indifferent support to the official party in the Church. The need of a united front to deal with the English Commissioners in 1642 helped in effecting a compromise settlement. Gillespie and Rutherfurd had an equal dread of schism and managed to control the zealots, but the agitation was such that the use of the Lord's Prayer in public worship gradually passed, for a time, out of the Church. In the negotiations preceding the Solemn League and Covenant, Gillespie played an active part, Henderson realising that this keen mind under guidance had valuable service to give to the Church. He was appointed in 1643 to the inner Committee of Moderators' Assessors, although not a Commissioner, because of Henderson's regard for him, and was one of those subsequently appointed to the Assembly Committee which helped to frame the Solemn League and Covenant. It was inevitable that he should be chosen as a Scottish Commissioner to Westminster.

At the Westminster Assembly, entrusted with the task of creating ecclesiastical standards for both nations, Gillespie made his most important contribution to Presbyterian history. The Scottish Commissioners, by insisting on being treated as National Commissioners, initiated propositions in Committee, debated them in Assembly, and still kept a revisory power in their hands by being Members of the Grand Committee of Parliament and Assembly which scanned the finished article before it ultimately was sent up to Parliament. Nevertheless every proposition had to pass before the keenest theological minds in England. In getting the standards shaped to the Scottish liking, the dominating factor was the keen debating power of Gillespie. Henderson's diplomacy and Rutherfurd's learning would have achieved far less but for Gillespie's debating acumen. The story of Westminster cannot be told in full here. One can only single out the prominent occasions in which Gillespie figured and these centre round the debate on Elders and the Erastian controversy.

The first matter to employ the talents of the Scots was naturally Church government and the form and nature of the Church to be established. They desired that this should be Presbyterian. English Presbyterianism had been amorphous, and loose in its ideas. The distinction between it and Congregationalism had not been clean cut, but, as Independency was hardening into a more rigorous congregational doctrine, the Scots in the Assembly now fought tooth and nail against the Independents for the rejection of Congregationalism and succeeded in bringing the English Presbyterians and some Episcopalians round to their side. In some matters, however, such as the nature of the Elder's office, they were nearer to the Independents than to their other English allies. It was in the matter of ascending courts that they fell foul of the Independents. Many of the English divines were reluctant to admit ruling elders to a full power in ecclesiastical courts. Tirelessly Gillespie pursued the debate using the proof texts, 1 Tim. 5.17, 1 Cor. 12.28, Rom. 12, with great dialectic skill. In the first draft of the propositions concerning Church government, adopted in 1645 by the whole Assembly, the compromise phrase, 'other church governors', was used instead of 'elders', but in the final Form of Church Government the term elders is also used. The Scots won their point in the end and a greater disciplinary power was vested in Kirk Sessions than the Englishman was keen to allow. They resented a 'lay' element in an ecclesiastical court.

Gillespie and Rutherfurd held that there was no such thing as a lay elder. Ordination had a less sacramental value to the Scots; it was a setting apart to office; elders and ministers were alike ordained servants of the Church, but ordained to different functions, one to preach and the other to rule. Gillespie's debating ability brought a good many of the Assembly into argument with the Scots' theory. He next went into the attack on the system of Church courts and extended himself in debate and pamphlet till the day was won in this matter also. He himself kept a journal of this debate, the most crucial of all for the Scots, and showed an amazing power of memorising all his opponent's argument and then rising to confute it trenchantly point by point. In 1645 he and Baillie had the happy task of bringing the results of their labours in the *Propositions of Church Government* and the *Directory of Public Worship* to the Scottish General Assembly in February, and having them passed, despite some opposition, by the Assembly. Gillespie drafted the Act which made them law in the Church.

The Erastian controversy began with the debate on the proposition, 'Pastors and teachers have power to enquire and judge who are fit to be admitted to the sacraments or kept from them, as also who are to be excommunicated or absolved from that censure.' The opposition to the proposition was comprised of the Independents and a small band of scholars, chiefly Hebraists, who were genuinely opposed to excommunication. The Independents opposed, not because they rejected the doctrine (their practice in New England showed them to be more rigorous indeed than the most die-hard Presbyterian), but because they feared its use as a weapon in Presbyterian hands and because they were anxious to win Parliamentary support. Their doctrine of excommunication amounted to congregational ostracism. Selden, the lawyer, a political Erastian, sought to prove that excommunication needed the consent of the civil power and was answered by Gillespie in a speech that destroyed his argument, excited the admiration of the whole Assembly, and even dragged a wry acknowledgement of defeat from Selden himself. For months the excommunication debate carried on. Gillespie along with Rutherfurd argued very strongly for a more summary procedure in excommunication than most of their colleagues favoured. Only on 3rd February 1645 was the *Directory for Excommunication* finished and sent to the Houses. It was never passed; instead an Ordinance was made cataloguing excommunicable sins; a further Ordinance enlarged the number of sins and appointed several commissioners in each shire to try the sinner before notifying him to the Eldership. To such a Church policy the Scots were bitterly opposed. The Assembly petitioned against the Ordinance. Parliament sulkily voted the petition a breach of privilege and sent some of her members to give the Assembly a dressing down. They were heard with dignity and answered with firmness. A whole spate of literature burst forth asserting the Church's right to be master in her own house, but the highlight of the controversy was the Gillespie-Coleman controversy.

A little space may be spared to elucidate this *bête noire* of Presbyterians. George Gillespie gave the word Erastian its modern meaning. Erastus himself was chiefly concerned with the repudiation of excommunication as a disciplinary weapon of the Church. He was only secondarily concerned with the magistrates' possible part in any such action. He was no Erastian as Prynne or Hobbes were Erastian. As was noticed, those who opposed Presbyterian excommunication at Westminster, the Independents for political reasons, the Hebraists for conscientious reasons, angled for Parliamentary support and got it to the extent that Parliament did intrude on the Assembly privilege of free debate and on the Church's claimed privilege of free discipline. Thus this matter of excommunication raised the whole matter of State control. The State held the Erastian view-point on excommunication. It was just a step to call those who supported the State's claim to control all ordinances Erastian, and so the word got its new meaning. No man flung it more viciously at his opponents than Gillespie; no man seems to have used excommunication more viciously either, for in *Nihil Respondes* he boasted, 'I dare say divers thousands have been kept off from the Sacrament in Scotland as un-

worthy to be admitted, where I myself have exercised my Ministry there have been some hundreds kept off, partly for ignorance
and partly for scandal.' Loving this weapon of authority, he was
most bitter against those who denied it. John Coleman, a competent Hebraist, and a fussy little man with an eye on the main
chance, had, in a sermon before Parliament, attacked the tenets of
the Excommunicators. Gillespie preached a few days after before
Parliament, made no reference in his sermon to Coleman, but
when he published his sermon added *A brotherly examination of
Mr Coleman's late printed sermon*. Coleman's retort drew the
caustic rejoinder from him, *Nihil Respondes or a Discovery of the
extreme Unsatisfactoriness of Master John Coleman's piece* (1655).
Coleman replied with *Male Dicis Maledicis* (1646), and Gillespie
made a scathing finish with *Male Audis or an answer to Mr Coleman
his Male Dicis*. Coleman died and that particular branch of the
controversy ended. He had been opposing Gillespie in the Assembly now debating the proposition in the Confession that 'Jesus
Christ as Head and King of His Church hath appointed a Government in the Church in the hands of Church Officers, distinct from
Civil Government'. Most vindictively in his preface to *Aaron's
Rod Blossoming* (1646) Gillespie writes of his death, 'The Lord was
pleased to remove him by death before he could do what he
intended to do in this and other particulars.' The Assembly
generously followed a stout controversialist to his grave, but I do
not think Gillespie went. The Coleman affair shows in Gillespie
the note of personal bitterness, even of malice, towards those who
differ from him or dare to answer him in his own coin, a note
which from now is to sound too often in the voice of a truly able
man. It can be attributed to some extent to failing health and to
a weary brain taxed with Assembly debates and the writing of his
last great work. Hussey, Coleman's friend, not unwarrantedly
hit back at Gillespie's vanity and his cultivation of an English
accent. *Aaron's Rod Blossoming* (1646) was intended to be
Gillespie's *magnum opus*. More expansive than his former works,
it elaborates the whole Scottish case for excommunication in the
historic justification. Book 1 deals with the Jewish Church

government and examines and confutes the case which Erastus made from it for excommunication by a *godly* magistrate. Book 2 tells of the origin and precepts of Erastianism and of the power and privilege of the magistrate in things and causes ecclesiastical. Book 3 is an exposition of the famous 'Tell the Church' passage and sundry other arguments. The whole is an ordered and learned exposition of his case.

Here perhaps one may refer to Gillespie's other literary labours at Westminster. He was indubitably the Scottish Pamphleteer, with a zest and ability for that somewhat dubious art. At least three anonymous pamphlets flew from his pen. The first was *A Late Dialogue betwixt a Civilian and a Divine* (1644)—a discussion of current affairs stating the ecclesiastical as opposed to the Parliamentary point of view. Gillespie is in a mood, for him, of reasonableness. He even shows some understanding of the English as opposed to the Scottish way of change. The English Civilian says, 'Sudden courses I doubt shall not so much glad us in the beginning as grieve us in the end.' The Scottish retort is that if change is needed, it may as well come 'suin as syne'. The war halts because England halts 'betwixt two or rather many opinions'. There is some clever twisting of Selden's tail and the Civilian is left unconvinced but meditative. His next essay at anonymous pamphleteering was an attack on John Goodwin's *Theomachia* (1644), a tract defending the Independent position with the robust vigour characteristic of the Ishmael of Coleman Street. Gillespie was not far behind with *Faces About or A Recrimination charged upon Mr John Goodwin in the point of Fighting against God and opposing the Way of Christ*. Recrimination it is, and Gillespie views with consternation the rise of religious toleration and commends Goodwin to Parliament's care as a mischief maker in no unsparing terms. In *Innocency's Triumph* Goodwin handled Gillespie as roughly: 'As for that empty pamphlet called *Faces About*, the author of it, whatever face or faces he had (for it may be he carries one in a hood), it seems he dare show none.' In fairness to Gillespie it can be said that policy rather than poltroonery dictated the anonymity of his tracts for he had an

abundancy of personal courage. He delved further into the toleration controversy with his next pamphlet, *Wholesome Severity reconciled with Christian Liberty or the True Resolution of a Present Controversy concerning Liberty of Conscience*. The work is the usual
vituperative pamphlet, but this controversy was largely left in
the hands of Baillie and Rutherfurd who wrote major works on
the subject. The game of both sides, Independent and Presbyterian, was to make the other as obnoxious to the State as possible,
and the spread of a weird sectarianism gave the Scots the opportunity to damn Independency as anti-social and anarchistic.
Gillespie said quite a lot on these lines in his two pamphlets on
the subject.

Two other works were written while he was at Westminster,
The Miscellany Questions and *The CXI Propositions*, concerning
the ministry and government of the Church. The treatise, *The
Miscellany Questions*, published posthumously in 1649, is a collection of notes made by Gillespie on all the questions that arose
during his stay at Westminster, perhaps made before going in or
after coming out of debate. They had been finally polished by
Gillespie himself with a view to publishing, but, death interven-
ing, they were published by his brother Patrick. They could be
best described as a series of ecclesiastical notes by an Assembly
debater, most useful for those who wanted to get the meat of the
question without reading Rutherfurd. *The CXI Propositions* were
an evil gift. In them he sets out all the ins and outs of the doctrine
of excommunication. He brought them to Scotland and presented them to the 1647 Assembly, had them approved in principle and sent down to Presbyteries and Universities for consideration. This doctrine and its more baleful practice was to play
havoc in the Church all through the next decade.

Gillespie at Westminster made an individual contribution to
the shaping of the Church of Scotland, apart from the fact that,
from the sheer brilliance of his debating power, he time and again
swung the Assembly round to the Scottish point of view. When
he is not ultra-controversial, any emendations he suggests make
for clarity and elucidation. Among everything else he, along

with Rutherfurd, gave the present doctrine of the eldership to the Scottish Church. Through his efforts the place of the Kirk Session as an integral court of the Church was finally established. The Scots at Westminster could not have done without him. Baillie's letters are filled with admiration for Mr George, 'that noble youth'. He wrote: 'Of a truth there is no man whose parts in a public dispute I so admire. He has studied so accurately all the points that ever yet came to our Assembly. He has gotten so ready, so assured, so solid a way of public debating, that however there be in the Assembly diverse very excellent men yet in my poor judgement there is not one speaks more rationally and to the point than that brave youth has done ever, so that his absence would be prejudicial to our whole cause and unpleasant to all that wishes it well.'[1] Gillespie's report to the General Assembly in 1647 is the best succinct account of the work at Westminster given by a contemporary divine, or by any other. He was not a theologian. The story that, in prayer, he conceived the answer to the question, 'What is God?' has been discredited, as Gillespie had left for Scotland before the matter came up in Assembly. He saved Patrick's life in London, for, by using considerable influence to save Will Murray—who had been caught—from being hanged as a spy, he preserved him to save Patrick from being hanged as a traitor. In 1645, in his journey north, he sought to preach the Scottish Army out of a mutiny at Newcastle, and a few months later he was again sent on a mission to withdraw that Army from Carlisle to Yorkshire.

Gillespie returned for the Assembly of 1647. Rutherfurd was in London, Henderson was dead, and he forthwith leapt into prominence as the nation's leading divine. Douglas was Moderator, but Gillespie was leading spirit. He steered the Confession of Faith through the Assembly. He composed a letter to the English Presbyterians exhorting them to be steadfast in their opposition to anti-Covenanting sectaries. He drew up the final Act which settled the old private meetings controversy. With Baillie he introduced the *Psalms* which were to be revised and

[1] Baillie, *Letters* ii, 159

authorised by a later Assembly. He maintained the power of Kirk Sessions in the teeth of Calderwood's opposition. He had all the documents and productions of the Westminster Assembly printed and published. He presented a gist of his *CXI Propositions on Church Government* to the Assembly and had them sent down, as noted, to Presbyteries and Assemblies. He was the 1647 Assembly. An act of Assembly inserted Gillespie's explicatory clause to Chapter 32 of the Confession. The power of Kings to convene Synods *pro re nata* for advice was allowed, but the intrinsic freedom of all ecclesiastical Assemblies resolutely asserted once and for all as the law of the Scottish Kirk. The passing of the Confession of Faith was his last great moment in a united Church.

The captive Charles was as great a problem to his keepers as his grandmother had been. The numerous intrigues in which he engaged cannot be recorded here, only the tentacle that reached out to embroil Scotland in the inky welter of the Engagement. The feudal party in Scotland were weary of ecclesiastical supremacy; there was in some quarters a reaction among moderate Covenanters to the policy which had delivered a native prince to another power. These and other circumstances gave rise to the 'Engagement', a secret treaty between Charles on the one hand and the Earls of Lauderdale, Lanark and Loudoun for the Scottish Estates. In return for the support of the Scottish Army, Charles agreed when restored to establish Presbyterianism and try it out for three years in England. When the treaty makers returned in 1648 to report to the Estates the storm broke. Argyll, Gillespie and Wariston who had had dealings with Charles before knew how little he was to be trusted. Much as they disliked the Cromwellian regime they were still in treaty with the English Parliament even though it was the Army's tool. The Church, a minority of the Estates and the bulk of the people were against any more adventures. The Commission of the Assembly moved into the attack asking information from the trio the moment they arrived home. A Declaration of the Engagement was presented to Parliament which drew much dry sarcasm. After protracted negotiations between Church and Parliament the latter, on 21st

April, published a Declaration stating they intended to take what action they pleased in regard to the Engagement. The Church's retort was *The Humble Representation of the Commission of the General Assembly to the Honourable Estates of Parliament.* It was, being Gillespie's, anything but humble and attacked the Engagers with a mordant and sarcastic irony, but we miss now the precision and clarity of his earlier works. The Declaration and Representation were read in all Churches throughout the land. The Estates' only retort, so weak was their power, was to send a letter to the Presbyteries asserting their superiority in matters political. The Church answered with the *Humble Vindication*, claiming that, as Parliament was disobeying the voice of God, the Church and Nation could disobey the voice of Parliament. Thus the affair dragged on till the Assembly of 1648. Gillespie was by now a dying man—others had been appointed to preach for him. He had been translated to the High Kirk on 22nd September 1647, the acknowledged place of an acknowledged leader. But the clear, precise, somewhat affected voice that had dominated Westminster was not strong enough for the rude atmosphere of the High Kirk with its congregation of hot-tempered barons, douce burghers and turbulent populace. Nevertheless, he was chosen Moderator in 1648. Baillie tells us he made a poor one.[1] He was ill and irritable. His keen debating mind caused him to enter into wordy contests with any members of the Assembly who differed from him and he was imperious to the point of bullying. Seldom able to moderate his own actions he was quite unable to moderate those of others. Argyll, Wariston and many Presbyterian leaders were absent. Many were playing safe. Gillespie courageously held the Kirk in her course of opposition to the Engagement when even his allies were failing him. But prolixity and irritation were common in the Assembly. Long drawn out Declarations against the Engagement show how Gillespie's mental powers are flagging. The Shorter and Larger Catechisms were approved, but the Directory for Church Government was attacked by Calderwood because of the Kirk Session propositions and its examination with

[1] Baillie, *Letters* iii, 53, 55, 62, 64 etc.

F

Gillespie's *CXI Propositions* remitted to the next Assembly. The *Psalms* were sent down to the Presbyteries for revision and report. The captious atmosphere delayed the passing of the last of the Westminster standards for not unnaturally the Assembly took its temper from its Moderator. Baillie's description of the Assembly is dispirited and sombre. He feared that new grounds of division were about to arise. He was right. Gillespie did not live to see these new contentions; his health was getting steadily worse, and he retired to Kirkcaldy in the hope that his native air might restore his strength. He died there on 17th December at the early age of thirty-five years. By then the Engagers' Army had been beaten at Preston. His last work was a short testimony dictated two days before his death in which he counselled the purging practice so disastrously put into effect by his party a month later in the Act of Classes. This was posthumously published along with a letter to the Commissioners of Assembly on 8th September and a short treatise comprised of sermon extracts called *A Useful Case of Conscience Discussed and Resolved concerning Associations and Confederacy with Idolaters.*

Gillespie wrecked the Engagement. If the Kirk could have been reasonably sure of Charles's promises being kept, disillusioned as her leaders were with the Cromwellian regime, they might have entered the battle on the Engagers' side on the grounds that the Rump had broken the Solemn League and Covenant. At one point in the negotiations between representatives of the Church and State, Lanark had well nigh won the Church round when Gillespie entered into the debate and turned the tide against him. Led by him the Church encouraged the boycott of supplies, discountenanced enlistment and deprived them of David Leslie as a general. Ill-led, ill-fed and semi-conscript, the Army's fate at Preston was a foregone conclusion. Lanark blamed Gillespie most of all for the fiasco. Yet Gillespie did what Henderson would have done. The people were war-weary, the land had suffered from Montrose's campaigns, Charles's word was utterly false and the Kirk knew it. To keep united and wait was the only practical course. So far he showed clear judgement and wise leadership, but he had not Henderson's gift of soothing hurt feelings and smoothing ugly disputes. Breaches between former allies were needlessly widened by his bitter tongue and even his friends could sometimes ill abide it. Never could it be said more truly that the evil men do lives after them. With his dying breath in that last publication he had ordered his Church to purge herself. His arrogant soul seems to have had a perverted delight in excommunication as a weapon of discipline. Desperately the Church carried out his dying orders. Engagers were excommunicated ecclesiastically, worse still, the Act of Classes was a political excommunication, and the strife engendered by this Act was to split the Kirk. Henderson led her out of bondage, the dying Gillespie led her into the wilderness.

Such was the career of Mr George Gillespie. He was the least lovable of the great quartet at Westminster. He was ambitious, vain and sly in ways unknown to Henderson and Rutherfurd. Clever and capable, he attracted attention and liked to attract it. 'No man was wont to find a greater attention and audience', says Baillie.[1] A triumph for a Scot at Westminster! The bitter tongue of his later years was due partly to failing health, partly to the super-sensitive temperament that goes with clever, vain people, and partly to the impatience with the intellectually inferior in whatever arena he might be confronted by them. Yet in his hey-day at Westminster his contemporaries smiled quietly as he preened himself and delighted in his success. He was a man all through and died fighting; he was upright in all his political conduct; he forsook no cause he sponsored. He gave of the uttermost he had, even to his life in the cause he served; if he never spared anyone, least of all did he spare himself. If the standards of government and worship ultimately framed at Westminster are predominantly Scottish in character, they owe that character to this young man who could so ably debate them through an Assembly of the age's most brilliant theological pundits. Twisse, Goodwin, Arrowsmith, Calamy, Marshall, Vines, Seaman, Burgess and Herle were not men to be readily browbeaten or easily

[1] Baillie, *Letters* iii, 12

convinced. His particular gift to us is, I think, the formulation of the Scottish doctrine of the Eldership and its powers. His fatal gift was the emphatic prominence he gave to the doctrine and practice of excommunication. He was a young man in his power, with the pride, the intolerance, the rashness, the courage, the unsparingness, the eagerness of youth. Baillie's is no bad epitaph: 'Certainly he was as able a man as our Kirk had; of a clear judgement, that which some misliked in him, would easily have been bettered by experience and years.'[1] His brother Patrick gained both and died with his armour tarnished. George Gillespie died with his sword drawn and his armour bright.

[1] Baillie, *Letters* iii, 68

CHAPTER VI

SAMUEL RUTHERFURD

SAMUEL RUTHERFURD was born about the year 1600 at Nisbet in the parish of Crailing. His father was, in all probability, a lesser laird of the district in fairly comfortable circumstances. Rutherfurd never speaks of any monetary difficulties during his own lifetime. He was educated most likely at Jedburgh, since he refers to the ignorant condition of the parish in which he was born; from there he went up to Edinburgh University. He may first have proposed studying law, but a letter written in 1636 says that for sixteen years he had desired to suffer for Christ so that some inward change or conversion must have taken place about 1620–21, the year of his graduation. After graduation his mind became set on the ministry and his appointment to the regentship of Humanity offered him further opportunity of study. He secured the regentship though his Latinity was inferior to that of another competitor, the examiners being assured of his 'pre-eminent abilities and virtuous disposition'.

Two years later he was forced to resign. Adamson, the Principal of the College, accused him of fornication to the Town Council, though no record exists to show that the charge was ever proved. Boyd had lately been dismissed and a regent who held his views was unwelcome to his successor, so Adamson seized the opportunity to force Rutherfurd out. It came when, acting contrary to College regulations, Rutherfurd married without the Principal's consent. Crawfurd, the historian of the College, writes, 'Mr Rutherfurd . . . having given some scandal in his marriage, was forced to demit the charge.' The Town Council paid him an 'honest gratification' at his demission. The whole business was 'framed' by the Episcopal party to oust Rutherfurd and have their own man appointed. Two things are significant.

In an age in which the past misdemeanours of a controversialist seldom escaped raucous flagellation, Rutherfurd's enemies—and they were many and vigorous—never refer to this 'scandal' and even pay tribute to the saintliness of his life while scourging his views and his party. In Letter CLXII, speaking of his own sins, he denies open outbreakings and his Edinburgh acquaintances were not such as would countenance the company or desire the spiritual counsels of a known fornicator.

The next few years are unrecorded but were far from barren. In them he made those personal contacts which determined the course of his whole life. He came to know Blair, Dickson, Livingstone and the evangelical coterie who were to do so much to overthrow Episcopacy. In 1627 the parish of Anwoth was disjoined by Sir John Gordon—later Viscount Kenmure—from the parish of Kirkmabreck to which it had been united and offered to Livingstone who refused it. Through John Ker of Prestonpans, a resolute opponent of the Perth Articles, Rutherfurd was appointed to the charge. This was one of those acts of policy by which the lairds were placing evangelical pastors in key positions. Situated on the high road between Dumfries and Stranraer, Anwoth was also near enough to Kirkcudbright for its minister to exercise an influence on burgh affairs. Its position makes the story of Archbishop Ussher's call on Rutherfurd not at all unlikely and the behaviour of both men on the occasion is quite in keeping with their character. Rutherfurd entered on his duties in the latter part of 1627. He never says how or when he was ordained. Wodrow says he gave no engagement to the Bishop, and Lady Kenmure's influence—she was a sister of Argyll—kept him relatively untroubled during the earlier part of his ministry. He was unremitting in his pastoral duties. The day, filled with studying, praying, preaching, teaching, visiting, was too short for him and he slept but six hours of it. Presbyterian propagandist, but first of all, Christian propagandist, his pastoral duty and Christian ministry were chiefest of his labours in Anwoth. His Communion seasons were attended from far and near, and his sermons have been preserved by an observer who took them down in shorthand. These occasions were used for the inculcation of Presbyterian doctrine and others were found. He was the prime instigator in the south-west of the 'conventicle' or private meeting and circulated a pamphlet, now lost, on the use and legality of such practices. This brought him into conflict with Sydserf, since 1634 Bishop of Galloway, one of Charles's new bishops, who was determined to extirpate the revolutionary Presbyterian 'cells' which he was finding in every parish in his diocese. Rutherfurd was summoned before the Synod on the charge of preaching treasonable doctrine in a sermon at Kirkcudbright. Summoned again before a court which Sydserf held at Wigtown, he was deprived of his ministerial office and sent to the High Commission Court in Edinburgh for sentence. There, further charges, based on his book against the Arminians, the *Exercitationes Apologeticae pro Divina Gratia*, were brought against him. He was deposed, forbidden to preach and banished to Aberdeen. But in the years in which he had laboured in Galloway, he had won the south-west to the Presbyterian cause and made it a decisive political and ecclesiastical influence in Scotland for over a century. In 1639, the petition opposing his translation to St. Andrews stated, 'the principal means whereby the body of gentry, at this time wanting a head, is united and stirred up, is some few ministers of whom he is the principal.' His influence long survived his death. Meantime, lonely and heartbroken, for he had lost his wife and children in Anwoth, he departed for Aberdeen.

He could not be kept silent. The loneliness of his spirit, the frustrated preaching instinct, the anxious zest for the spiritual welfare of his flock, broke forth in that outpouring of letters with which his name is forever associated. The greatest volume of his letters comes from Aberdeen, for after 1639 he was too busily employed in public affairs. The letters have been praised for their passionate Christology and vilified for their eroticism; but acquaintance with the writers of the seventeenth century shows this eroticism to be technical rather than integral, springing from the conception of the Church as the Bride of Christ and from an allegoric interpretation and use of the Song of Solomon. The same sort of imagery will be found in many of the religious poets and divines of the age. Adverse criticism can easily magnify a literary convention into an indecency; even then there are few passages that can be so magnified and only sixty out of two hundred and eighty letters from Aberdeen are written to women. Unable to preach, the exile evangelised by letter. Nobles, merchants, lawyers, lairds, farmers, cottagers, burghers, ministers, ladies of high degree, mothers in their sorrow, all sorts and conditions of men and women, with no respect of persons, received letters from him, some warning, some comforting, some expounding, some exhorting, some rebuking, but all speaking of the glory of Christ. The Person of the Redeemer fills the Letters. Rutherfurd was no erotic mystic but a man in trouble who had come to lean closely on Christ. At the same time as he commends Christ to his reader, he commends the Presbyterian cause as Christ's cause, but it is with the development of a man's or a woman's life in Christ, through joy, sorrow, doubt or fear, through all human experience, with which he is most concerned. No Scotsman has surpassed him in his wealth of imagery or in the richness and aptness of religious epigram. While he was still in Aberdeen, his letters were being collected and passed round the conventicles in the south-west where his prestige as a martyr enhanced their power as propaganda. Even in Aberdeen he found scope for controversy, disputing with Dr Baron the nature of the ceremonies—a dispute in which both men claimed the victory.

The signing of the National Covenant released him from his exile and he returned to Anwoth in February 1638. In June of that year, being in Edinburgh, he greeted Hamilton's arrival with a sermon which 'felled the fourteen bishops and houghed the ceremonies', and which his own party noted as being remarkably outspoken. He attended the succeeding Assembly which abolished the Bishops and from then on appeared among the Kirk's leaders in committee and council. At the Assembly of 1639, he was translated to St. Andrews as Professor of Divinity, a post which he was genuinely reluctant to accept. To overcome this reluctance he was at the same time appointed colleague in the ministry to

Robert Blair, that he might exercise fitly his pastoral gifts. The Presbyterianism of St. Andrews was regarded as dubious and Rutherfurd was appointed to restore it to Melville's orthodoxy and 'to make many able ministers'.

Before the preacher becomes submerged in the polemicist and the professor, a short word may be said about his sermons. These have been preserved in two volumes edited by the late Dr Bonar, *Fourteen Communion Sermons* and *Quaint Sermons hitherto unpublished*, and in the *Trial and Triumph of Faith, Christ Dying and Drawing Sinners to Himself* and the unique *Power and Prevalency of Faith and Prayer*. There are also his two Westminster Sermons before the Lords and Commons. He is one of Scotland's greatest preachers. Christ and sinful man is the central theme of his preaching which transcends the hard bounds of his theology so that he joyously and unconsciously approaches the 'universalism' which his lectures so vigorously damned. 'If ye ask for whom Christ died, I answer, "for all that lean to Him, be they whom they will." Take "ay" to you till Christ say "I died not for you." A cord is cast down into a hollow pit to draw up you and a hundred more nor you. If ye dispute "is the cord cast down for me?" I will tell you how ye shall answer that doubt. Grasp and hold fast by it for your life and out of question it was cast down for you. If ye take the offer, question not His goodwill. Step in. Christ's goodwill will not ask to whom pertain ye.' (*Communion Sermons*, p. 303.) Few Scotsmen, in prose or verse, have possessed such a wealth of imagery. His sermons are full of inspired and graphic word painting. The home, the farm, the fisheries, sport, war, the law, every art and part of life which he touched supply him with apt analogy to drive home the spiritual truth. As his people listened, they must have seen not only Christ, but the very life around them with different eyes. The man whom Taylor Innes accuses of knowing nothing about children, is full of metaphors from child life, metaphors that reveal the hunger of a man who has lost many, for a child of his own. Plain speaking abounds to peer and peasant, for Rutherfurd, like Luther, believed that a sermon should have teeth. If disciplined and orderly thought had balanced the intensity of his spirit and the wealth of his imagery, as a preacher he would have had few rivals in any age. The power of his pulpit won the south-west to his cause in his early ministry and the power of his pen held it true to whichever side he supported all through his life.

From 1639 until 1643 when he set out for Westminster, Rutherfurd was mostly employed with the work of his professorship. It was inevitable that he should be embroiled in the 'novations' controversy, which occupied the attention of three succeeding Assemblies and which by its threat to internal peace further strengthened Henderson's desire for complete Presbyterian uniformity. An ultra-puritan party had grown up in the Kirk which objected to certain features in public worship, hitherto prevalent or at least allowed—read prayers, the use of the Lord's Prayer, the use of the Gloria Patri and the ministers bowing or kneeling in private prayer before the service began. When the minister ceased to be *persona grata* to the local saints, they employed against him the same practices as had been used against the Episcopalian; they assembled themselves in conventicles or private meetings where the 'faithful' were encouraged and the minister's life and conduct were deplored. A meeting at the house of the Laird of Leckie brought matters to a head. Leckie in his prayers commented pithily on the life and doctrine of Mr Henry Guthrie, his minister. Guthrie and the magistrates of Stirling sought to suppress the meetings and the whole affair was brought before the 1640 Assembly at Aberdeen. Rutherfurd, who had already defended private meetings, proceeded to do so now. In the end, to secure peace, he gave way and agreed to an Act which limited conventicle worship to the members of one family, asserted the lawfulness of read prayers and stated that only the minister should expound Scripture. In 1641 the Assembly decided, with naïve dogmatism, that conventicles in former times had been very profitable, but now, under a settled ministry, were 'inexpedient, unlawful and schismatical'. Independency hydra-headed was rising on the ecclesiastical horizon, so Rutherfurd and his friends surrendered in the interests of Presbyterian authority, though the extremists remained malcontent and survived to become the nucleus of the Remonstrant and later the Protester party. At St. Andrews too Rutherfurd found trouble. Howie, the Principal, had mismanaged the College rents and Rutherfurd complained to the Estates and a Committee was appointed to investigate. Howie resigned, but the case was one only of administrative incapacity, for, at the 1641 Assembly, Henderson secured Howie his stipend for life.

So the years passed till the event of the Solemn League and Covenant. Rutherfurd, a member of the inner circle of the Kirk's councils, was an intimate of Henderson, Wariston and Argyll; his reputation as a scholar was unequalled save by that of George Gillespie. When the project of sending four divines to Westminster was first mooted, Robert Blair was the original fourth, but Rutherfurd was substituted in his place. Blair was, perhaps, unwilling to go and the scholarship of Rutherfurd gave him a claim above all others to represent Scotland at such an Assembly. Blair had been selected in 1641 to deal with ecclesiastical questions related to Independency. Yet nothing appears to have come from his pen. In 1642 Rutherfurd published his *Peacable Plea for Paul's Presbyterie in Scotland*, a mild and temperate statement of the Presbyterian doctrine of the Church, in membership and ministry, set over against the tenets of Independency, which further singled him out for the journey to Westminster.

At Westminster, among the best scholars of the age, he established a reputation rivalled by few members of that Assembly. Wherever the conflict was hottest, Rutherfurd and Gillespie were to be found. 'Mr Rutherfurd spoke . . . and there was a long debate'; how often in Lightfoot's Journal we find these phrases side by side! Time and again his scholarship and Gillespie's rhetoric swung the Assembly round to the Scottish Presbyterian doctrine and practice in the drafting of the 'Form and Order of Church Government' and of the 'Directory for the Public Worship of God'. Occasionally the brothers in arms differed, as when Rutherfurd with most of the Englishmen held out for the child's right to baptism apart from any rigorous examination of the parents' moral fitness. With Gillespie, he upheld the Assembly in resisting Parliamentary interference and engaged bitterly in the 'Erastian controversy' which sprung up through their action. As the sects in England became more numerous, and noisy, he took part in the vitriolic anti-toleration controversy which arose. Volume after volume flowed from his pen and he spoke as fearlessly at Westminster as he did in the Galloway glen. His *Lex Rex* was the first statement of Scottish democracy in the native tongue. Based on an earlier treatise on *Defensive War*, it laid down the principles governing the responsibility of King and Parliament to the people and showed no great love for a Second Chamber. 'I see not what privilege Nobles have above Commons in a court of Parliament.' It asserted the doctrines of limited monarchy and the duty of the King to guide his ministers and be an example of gracious morals as the most eminent servant of the State. It is filled with many acute political apothegms but constant comparison of Charles and his Queen with Ahab and Jezebel brought him to the verge of the scaffold which he escaped only by death. He played no small part in framing the Westminster Confession of Faith and sponsored Twisse's form of Calvinism with its supralapsarian emphasis on election, displacing the older Calvinism of Rollock with the emphasis on calling.

At first, he was happy in London; his second wife, Jean McMath, was with him; he enjoyed the company of the greatest scholars of the age both in the Assembly and at many a friendly supper party. Sorrow came at the end. His two children died and he himself fell ill through overwork; the gulf between Independent and Presbyterian widened and bitterness increased. Yet when he left London in 1647, with the idea of a united Church further off than ever, he had been in no small way responsible for setting up the world-wide basis and standards of the Presbyterian Churches of the future.

He came back to a Scotland in which Presbyterianism was triumphant and the Kirk busily engaged in setting her affairs in order. The Westminster standards were carefully gone over in the Assemblies of 1647, 1648 and 1649 and became the law and practice of the Kirk. Gillespie, untiring in his efforts, secured their speedy adoption and spent himself to ultimate exhaustion. Rutherfurd took up and pursued unremittingly the cause of the popular election of ministers until he had election by the congregation made the law of the Kirk in 1649. Abolished at the Restoration, this law was restored at the Revolution but repealed in 1712. At the time many of his contemporaries considered this action an undue approach to Independency.

Charles, now in bondage, was still a menace to peace. By 1647, he was ready to promise anything to anybody and the Earls of Lanark, Lauderdale and Loudoun, on behalf of the Scottish Estates, entered into the 'Engagement' with Charles. In return for sanction of the Solemn League and Covenant, the establishment, on trial, of Presbyterianism in England for three years and a verbal pledge of the incorporation of some of the northern English counties in the Kingdom of Scotland, the Scots pledged themselves to invade England in Charles's support if Parliament did not restore him to his privileges, among them the control of the militia and the power of veto in Parliamentary legislation. The tale can be briefly told for the effects of the Engagement are more important than the military fiasco. Some in the Kirk, with proper safeguards, might have lent support to Charles, but few now trusted his word. The country was weary of war and the Kirk opposed to it, as was a minority of the Estates, headed by Argyll and Wariston. The supporters of the Engagement were the feudal chiefs, suspicious of the Kirk's rise to power and desirous of checking it. In boycotting the Engagement, the Kirk had the support of the country and Loudoun deserted to the Kirk party. Ill led, for Leslie would not act as general, ill fed, for the people had no desire for war, the army of the Engagers perished at Preston. Cromwell entered Edinburgh; Argyll's party rose to power and the Act of Classes was passed. By it civil and religious penalties of varying degree were inflicted on the unfortunates who fought for Charles; in various 'classes', according to the nature of their 'crime', their estates were forfeited or they were fined and all were disqualified from holding office in the State for varying periods of years. No blood was shed except Hamilton's by Cromwell but the vindictive categorising of the noble offenders caused them to exact their pound of flesh when the King came home. Rutherfurd gave whole-hearted support to the Act.

The execution of Charles complicated Scottish loyalties. It was one thing to hold a King and Scotsmen in duress till he came to terms—indeed it was an old Scots custom—but it was another thing to cut his head off. Kirk and State reacted in revolt and all but a few extremists condemned the deed. Rutherfurd was neither a regicide nor a republican; though he held that kings might be deposed, he favoured a limited monarchy. After delay, dubious diplomacy, the tragedy of Montrose's invasion and execution, Charles II came to Scotland after having taken the Covenants. In imposing them on Charles, the leaders of the Kirk, from past experience, were within their rights in seeing that what had been won was safeguarded, and the greater hypocrisy lay with the King who took them with his tongue in his cheek and with a Buckingham for his counsellor. But royal oaths were insufficient to create an army able to meet and beat Cromwell, for many of the best field officers had been debarred from service by the Act of Classes. Bad field officers cost David Leslie the field of Dunbar in September 1650 and the recruiting problem became more accentuated than ever. The western Covenanters, imputing Dunbar as a divine judgement on Charles, drew up the 'Remonstrance' in which they damned the whole policy of the Estates and renounced all part in any military adventures in support of the King. This marked the parting of Argyll and Wariston for the latter was behind the Remonstrance though he denied drafting it. Argyll, having crowned him, was pledged to the support of the Covenanted King. Rutherfurd, in a dilemma as to whom to follow, loyally, but reluctantly, went with Argyll, though opposed to any dealings with those debarred by the Acts of Classes and to their appointment to office. Although he was not a Remonstrant, his sympathies were with them and the repeal of the Act of Classes together with the Kirk's adoption of the 'public Resolutions' finally drove him back to the western camp.

The Estates, from January 1651 to May of that year, had persistently sought a deliverance from the Commission of Assembly on the matter of the Act and of the admission of the Engagers, so that the 'public Resolutions for the defence of the Realm' might have practical force through gaining the Kirk's support and finally the Commission in a somewhat oracular decision gave its support. Engagers might be admitted provided they satisfied the Kirk, and provided that there was no victimisation of anti-Engagers. The Commission also ordered Presbyteries to deal with any who opposed the Resolutions and summon them to the next General Assembly in July 1651. The storm broke. Rutherfurd was furious at what he believed was a betrayal of the Kirk and the democrat in him revolted at the Commission's assumption of an Assembly's powers. At the Assembly in 1651 he entered the famous 'Protest', outlined by Wariston, absent through fear of arrest, and worked over by himself. The protest was not directed so much at the Commission's findings, with which, of course, he and Wariston utterly disagreed, but very ably attacked the legality of the Assembly called to sanction them, the chief objection being that in debarring the anti-Resolutioners and Remonstrants, the Commission had prelimited elections—as undoubtedly it had. The King's letter and the Lord High Commissioner's speech were made further grounds for complaint. During the Assembly, Cromwell won his second victory of the campaign at Inverkeithing and the Assembly moved from St. Andrews to Dundee. Rutherfurd continued in his assertion of the nullity of the Assembly's authority and although the Assembly processed and deposed Patrick Gillespie, Guthrie, Simpson and other 'Protesters' the Resolutioners were too politic to cast out so great a name as his from the Assemblies of the Kirk.

The unity of the Kirk was gone and a fierce pamphlet warfare broke out between the parties. In James Guthrie, Patrick Gillespie and Wariston, the Protesters had easily the best pamphleteers, for Robert Douglas and the veteran David Dickson were no match for them—till they brought in James Sharp. In a sense, this split apparently created by the political situation had existed since 1641 and the 'novations' controversy. The extreme ultra-Puritan party had clamoured then for 'purity' of worship; the same men, influenced by the work of George Gillespie and Rutherfurd, now demanded 'purity' in the membership of the Kirk and the casting out of all 'malignants' and their supporters. They had had their purging way in the Act of Classes and now they opposed the moderate tendencies of Douglas as they had formerly opposed those of Henderson in their earlier controversy. In one aspect the contest was a struggle between the ultra-puritan and the moderate puritan; neither side had the sole prerogative of evangelical preaching, for if Rutherfurd cast in his lot with the 'Protesters', David Dickson was with the other side. When the political issue became obscure and unimportant through Cromwell's ascendancy and the abolition of the General Assembly, the conflict, on the popular level, became one between men of differing religious temperament rather than between men of different ecclesiastical views; on the higher level it deteriorated into a scrambling intrigue for Cromwell's favour by the leaders of the two parties.

The Assembly met in July 1652 and again the 'Protesters' asserted its illegality and the illegality of the preceding Assembly. In 1653 the Assembly met, to meet no more for many years. By the command of the Protector and his Council, the meeting was dispersed by the military as was also a meeting of 'Protesters' called to protest against the Assembly. The next seven years of the Kirk's history lack the dignity and sincerity of her immediate past and it took the years of persecution to restore her integrity. Cromwell governed Scotland through a Council of State and both 'Protesters' and 'Resolutioners' soon began intriguing for place and for power for their faction. Efforts at reconciliation were rendered fruitless by the clash of antipathetic personalities, Wariston and Guthrie especially provoking bitter opposition from Dickson and Sharp on the other side. Wariston sometimes deliberately wrecked peace proposals and ultimately became Cromwell's paid tool. Patrick Gillespie accepted the Principalship of Glasgow University from Cromwell's hands. Men who had fearlessly braved Charles now trailed the ante-chambers of the Lord Protector. Rutherfurd, while retaining his Protester convictions, became sick of the whole business.

By 1655 he ceased to take an aggressive part in the wrangling and intrigues of the two parties and sought to escape from the internecine tragedy in penning works of practical divinity and in vigorously combating in the lecture room the Arminianism which he had hated all his life. The fruit of these years was *The Covenant of Life Opened* (1655), *The Influences of the Life of Grace* (1659), *The Power and Prevalency of Faith and Prayer Evidenced* (1703 posthumously) and *Examen Arminianismi* (1668 posthumously). These later works lack the freshness and vigour of the letters and sermons, but they contain passages which glow with the old spirit; the *Power and Prevalency* especially, written with the humility of a deepened experience, reveals the unquenchable faith dwelling in that racked body and tortured mind and was the last clear flame of the man whose soul indeed was the candle of the Lord, although like all candles it sometimes burned with a smoky fire. The *Examen* shows no weakness in his power of dialectic and is more lucid and orderly than much of his other polemic. *The Survey of Mr Hooker's Sum of Church Discipline* written in 1650 was published in 1658 and incurred the bitter criticism of the Resolutioners because in a lately added preface he asserted that inferior synods could disobey higher courts if these courts commanded anything contrary to the Word of God. His opponents were not altogether wrong in charging him with certain leanings towards the Independency which he so furiously attacked.

His later life in St. Andrews was spent in controversy with his colleagues because of the unhappy split in the Kirk, and he became lonely and cut off from the fellowship he had so much enjoyed, from Blair, Wood and Jamieson, colleagues and once intimate friends. Even his early days had begun in strife. He was sent to St. Andrews as a professor in 1639 to wean it from Episcopal nurture. McWard, his pupil, most disloyally calls his Alma Mater 'the very nursery of all superstition in worship and error in doc-

G

trine and the sink of all profanity in conversation among the students'. It is pleasing to note that Rutherfurd nowhere so reviles the College of which he was Principal. He was appointed Rector not long after his arrival to deal with Principal Howie's mismanagement and had to petition the Estates before affairs were settled. Henderson, a St. Andrews man, took Howie's part against the Edinburgh 'new broom' and Howie was maintained in his position and his rents secured to him. Rutherfurd for three years received no stipend from the landward parish of which he had pastoral care and his professor's salary was at the beginning insecure. He had no easy time and for three years the burden of teaching and administration of St. Mary's fell on him till Alexander Colville was appointed professor in 1642 and James Wood in 1645. He succeeded Howie as Principal in 1647 and for a few years there was harmony in the College. Then came the Public Resolutions and the resulting disputes, which drove Wood to St. Leonard's, of which he became Principal and gave Rutherfurd in his dying hours James Sharp as a colleague. Yet, so great was the trust in his integrity and the respect for his ability, that the Resolutioners never seriously sought to remove Rutherfurd from the Principalship of St. Mary's, not even to please Oliver Cromwell. Rutherfurd on his part refused a twice offered invitation to a chair in Utrecht and another to one in Harderwyck, tempting though the unhappiness and insecurity of the time must have made them. He remained a resolute opponent of Cromwell and St. Andrews received no benefit from the Cromwellian regime.

As a professor he pleased some and displeased others. The *Examen* shows he could lecture with lucidity and system. McWard found him the paragon of professors, another student, a later conformist, found him confused in thought and method; perhaps the heat of controversy sometimes sidetracked the main trend of his lecture. Principal, Professor, Politician, and speculative Theologian, he never lost touch with the humble world about him. By letter, lecture and life he drove home to his students the supreme importance of their pastoral ministry, and in that crowded life of his own diligently performed the work of country minister in the landward part of the parish, receiving little stipend for the work, for years remaining unpaid and unprotesting. 'Our Mr Rutherfurd seemed to be many able godly men or one who was furnished with the grace and abilities of many.' As a preacher he was, till the dark days, in great demand at every Communion season in Fife. When he, Blair and Wood disagreed and the other two became Resolutioners, Rutherfurd refused to serve at the Communion table with them, but at the end they became reconciled.

His end was not far off. Cromwell died and Charles returned and remembered the humiliating oaths, the long sermons, the men who had lectured on the duties of kings and the man who had written of his father and mother as Ahab and Jezebel. James Sharp, sent home from London by the restored Rump Parliament with instructions to attend to his pastoral duties and keep out of politics, had no intention of obeying their instructions. Suspected of trafficking with Charles he was soon in touch with Monk who had hitherto had little to do with him. He assisted the general to draft the proclamation made to the Army at Coldstream on its march south and was soon in London with him. All knew that Charles would be restored; but on what terms? Extremists such as Guthrie would have no king whatever. Moderate Protesters were willing to accept a king sworn to *both* Covenants, and the Resolutioners agreed with them. Only the obstinacy of a few Protesters kept the parties apart. Efforts towards union were made with last-minute desperation. Rutherfurd was prepared to accept them provided all censures were removed from the Protesters. Time alone was needed to unite the two parties and even very little of that, but they never got it. Sharp again in London with Crawfurd, Lauderdale and Glencairn eventually crossed to deal with Charles at Breda. The Protesters tried to have Robert Douglas and the Resolutioners subscribe with them to a petition against the establishment of Episcopacy in England. Douglas had by now abandoned the idea of pressing the Solemn League and Covenant and refused, conveying to them a veiled warning which he had received from Sharp who had written to him, 'The Protesters will not be welcome here, their doom is dight.' It was. Charles returned. Argyll was arrested. Wariston fled. On 23rd August Guthrie and the leading Protesters were arrested when holding a meeting in Edinburgh. On 31st August 1660 Sharp returned with a letter from Charles to the Presbytery of Edinburgh promising to preserve the government of the Church of Scotland and intimating that another General Assembly would be called. It never was called; the feudal party with their bitter memories and old grudges were now in power and had no intention of surrendering it to a dominant Assembly. Parliament met on 1st January 1661. Act after Act destroyed the old Covenanting legislation. The Act Recissory rendered null and void all achievements in Church and State of the past twenty years. By an Act of 6th September 1661 Episcopacy was made the form of Church government in Scotland. Its establishment was aided by the fatal divisions of the Church, but it was mainly brought about by the desertion of the feudal nobility from the Presbyterian cause. Desire for power, hope of English preferment, reaction against a harsh discipline were all motives in the betrayal. Sharp, part Judas, part Demas, was their tool.

Ill health and dislike of the Protector had kept Rutherfurd in retirement between 1658 and 1660 but when Guthrie was arrested he would have dragged himself to die by his side. Guthrie had tightened the noose round his neck by writing a petition to Charles, reminding him of his promises and demanding the establishment of the true religion. Rutherfurd wrote to his friends in the south-west asking them to send a similar petition, but making it clear that he had never had dealings with Cromwell and that he had always favoured the idea of a limited monarchy— very limited indeed to a Stuart. About the same time a petition for the release of the imprisoned Protesters was framed for them to sign in which they would renounce the Remonstrance. Rutherfurd's opinion of this petition was asked; he condemned it, and though never a Remonstrant, stated clearly that he agreed with Guthrie and the others in their first petition. It may have been a trap. All the others, except Guthrie, were set free. On

15th September the Committee of Estates ordered all copies of *Lex Rex* to be handed to the Crown Solicitor before October; some were burned publicly in Edinburgh, some at the gates of his own College. He was deprived of all his University offices and his pastoral charge. His stipend was confiscated and he was summoned to appear before the Committee of Estates on a charge of treason. He was too ill to appear and a summons to appear before Parliament came in March 1661. To the messengers the dying man replied with all his old courage, with the democratic arrogance that dwelt in a man in other ways so humble. 'I have got a summons already before a superior Judge and Judicatory and it behoves me to answer my first summons, and ere your day arrive I shall be where few kings and great folks come.' He died on the evening of the day on which the Act Recissory was passed.

Rutherfurd's work for the Covenanting Reformation was as great as that of Henderson though less apparent. He largely created and held together, even from Aberdeen the south-west party which contributed dominantly to the success of the 1638 revolution, and was an active and dictating power in the politics of the next fifty years, even when bloodily bruised by Dalziel's ruffians and Claverhouse's dragoons; for that party's violent resistance to Charles and James made it impossible for William to achieve any other than a Presbyterian settlement in Scotland, whereas in Ireland Tory opposition frustrated his attempts to reward the Presbyterians for their loyalty, by defeating the Toleration Act with which he sought to give them a recognised status. Rutherfurd's ultra-Calvinism and radical democracy both became the cherished possession of burgher, farmer and peasant in the south-west. He did not sign the Remonstrance but the Remonstrants and the subsequent Protesters were the natural crop of his sowing. To them *Lex Rex* was an inspired call to resistance and no dead letter. There was political consideration as well as personal venom in the last indignity which recalled and burned as many copies as could be found. Right up to the beginning of this century you would find men of his creed in Galloway.

My maternal ancestors have been tenants in the same farm since at least 1590. They were Cameronians and Wodrow tells of their torture and exile. In my possession are books handed down in the family, and they are volumes of Rutherfurd and Twisse. I can remember a grandfather who represented the old traditions of hard Calvinism and political Radicalism. In these old Galloway families at the beginning of this century and the end of the last the Irish Question drove a wedge between these allegiances and made the Radical who placed his Protestantism first either a Unionist or a non-voter. I can remember people in these old families who always talked of 'worthy Mr Rutherfurd' and 'the learned "Mattha" Henry' with simple and reverent awe. In Galloway when I was a boy the wind that blew over Airds Moss could still be heard 'soughing' in the hills and Establishment and Free Church would together worship yearly at the Monument hill in Anwoth or at the even more remote and lonely graves of the martyrs that graced the grey-brown Galloway hills.

Rutherfurd was as determined in his opposition to the Engagers as Gillespie, as merciless and as mistaken in his advocacy of excommunication for what was a political miscarriage rather than a religious offence. But he considered that the Engagers broke the Solemn League and Covenant. The same consideration made him reject any dealings with Cromwell when he ruthlessly shattered every one of its sacred articles. He withdrew from the Protesters when they began to deal with the Usurper. He was consistent to the oath he had taken, long after that Covenant had ceased to be practical politics, and though dead, was the inspiration of the small party that would have imposed both Covenants on William and Mary.

He was the greatest and most learned of Scotland's theologians and, as will be seen, introduced and promulgated the doctrines of supralapsarian Calvinism in Scotland, but his influence is more seen in our now accepted theories and practices of Church government. Rutherfurd was the great apologist of Presbyterianism. Neither Henderson nor Gillespie would have been adequate at Westminster without him. He defended with his learning the postulates of the former, and with it supplied the propaganda of the latter. Much that he framed and defended has passed permanently into the framework of the Scottish Church, although it took two centuries to establish some of his proposals which went further than anything laid down in the Books of Discipline. He believed that a congregation should elect its own pastor, and by 'congregation' he meant not only heads of families, but every adult in it. 'Nor are women, sons, servants, debarred from voicing in an election,' he wrote in the *Survey*, and as was seen he established popular election for a time, as the law of the Church. Its abolition in 1712 was the root cause of the Disruption. He asserted the principle of the Barrier Act long before its day. In the *Peacable Plea* he announced that 'matters to be enacted by General Assemblies are to be first referred to congregations and elderships of particular congregations'. He established the doctrine that profession of faith is the only basis of membership of the Church visible, and in his doctrine of Baptism made this profession the only demand upon the parents and sponsors vesting the child's right to the sacrament in the 'federal holiness' of the nation, that he or she was born in a professedly Christian land. Despite efforts by Boston of Ettrick and later by others, to establish a more puritan and exclusive practice, Rutherfurd's doctrine has remained the law of the Church and was re-emphasised at the General Assembly of 1951. The power and position of the elder, somewhat vaguely defined before 1638, was by him and Gillespie finally established as now we know it in the Scottish Church, but they must bear the blame for underlining the harsh discipline of excommunication which begot unfortunate political results. More than any other, Rutherfurd vindicated, expounded and nationalised the principles underlying the Scottish Presbyterianism of the Books of Discipline. His learning was encyclopaedic, his memory inexhaustible, and his zeal indefatigable. When theological defence was a conditional necessity of his Church's existence, he was her greatest defender.

Much has been written about the puzzling dualism of Rutherfurd's nature. He was an intensely passionate man and an intensely involved thinker. When he wrote of Christ to his people, every aspect of His glory had to be revealed; when he became involved in an argument, every facet of the case had to be reviewed. Contradictions in his thought can only be explained by his passion for pushing an argument to the extreme. His mysticism was in measure rhetorical, for he expatiated on the person of Christ by letter and sermon to an expectant audience, of which he was acutely conscious, but his private life was filled with long hours of quiet devotion and deep meditation on his Saviour's glory. His own faith was a personal adherence to Christ—not a mere zealous assent to a creed. He was, at one and the same time, irascible and forgiving in personal matters; only when ecclesiastical principles were involved did he become dour and intractable. He was completely unworldly in financial affairs and gladly sacrificed health, wealth and life to the cause for which he fought. He was loved in his parish and by his friends and even to the last, respected by all but the most inveterate of his opponents. Towards the end of his life he wrote, 'I will neither lead nor drive except I see Christ's love run in my channel, and when I wait and look for Him the Upper Way I see His wisdom is pleased to play me a slip and come the Lower Way.' As the shadows lengthened and strengthened he became a humbler and wiser man, but he walked with the same courage in the Valley of the Shadow of Death as he walked in the high Halls of Westminster and, dying, he lighted others through the ensuing gloom till a better day broke upon his Church.

From the storm and sunshine, the success and the sorrow of these men who made the Second Reformation, all of whom died in some sad hour of crisis, the last, Rutherfurd, in the most tragic of all, we turn to consider the missionary effort of the Church of Scotland at Westminster. The Westminster standards, as formulated, were a triumph of Scottish ecclesiastical propaganda. Had Parliament prevailed instead of the Army, some form of Presbyterianism might have become established in the Anglican Church. The Scots fought an intense battle outside as well as inside the Assembly, for they realised that Assemblies are as susceptible as individuals to public opinion. They succeeded in London in creating a favourable opinion to the Presbyterian cause which, in no small way, shaped the course of events in the Assembly. Cromwell wrecked the immediate establishment of the Westminster formulas in England, but the Scots directed the Assembly into the creation of those standards which have been the basic foundation of all English-speaking Presbyterian Churches.

CHAPTER VII

THE WESTMINSTER ASSEMBLY

THE SOLEMN LEAGUE AND COVENANT gave the Scots the opportunity of pursuing their Presbyterian ideal of religious uniformity within Britain; indeed, as early as 1641 they began to plan their campaign which aimed at securing the co-operation of the English Parliament in the overthrow of Episcopacy. The religious establishment now to be set up was to be propounded by an Assembly of Divines and sanctioned by the General Assembly and by the Parliaments of both Kingdoms. England had already set up such an Assembly at Westminster and to its number were added seven Scots as Commissioners, four divines and three elders. Alexander Henderson, Samuel Rutherfurd, Robert Baillie, George Gillespie were the ministers; Sir Archibald Johnston of Wariston, Lord Maitland (Lauderdale), and the Earl of Cassillis were the elders. Cassillis never sat but the Earls of Argyll and Loudoun and Lord Balmerino later took part in the Assembly's proceedings. To this body was now entrusted the framing of the standards of faith, worship and Church government which were to unite the whole country. Dr Mure Mackenzie in her *Passing of the Stewarts* states that this preponderantly English Assembly gave its standards to the Church of Scotland, the implication being that these are thus of English and alien origin. It would be much more accurate to say that these Scotsmen brought a preponderantly English Assembly to accept what were in the main the Scottish positions in all matters of Church order, government and worship. There was no royal ukase, Crown agent or subservient hierarchy to back them; their achievements were the result of diligent propaganda, weighty scholarship and keen debate in the Assembly itself which the next four chapters will seek to show.

The Assembly was in existence when the Scots arrived and debating the Thirty-Nine Articles in a desultory fashion. It had been mooted as early as September 1642, when the Commons discussed a request from the Scottish General Assembly for the abolition of Episcopacy. The House then resolved that Episcopal government was 'a great impediment to the perfect reformation and growth of religion, and very prejudicial to the state and government of this kingdom and that the same shall be taken away'. After much debate and frustrated legislation an Assembly of divines was set up by an Ordinance of 12th June 1643 to advise Parliament and assist in establishing a settled form of religion. What that form was to be was difficult to determine. In England, Episcopacy had become hated and distrusted for various political and economic reasons outwith the scope of the present argument; but many still loved the accepted worship of the Church, had no desire to see it abolished and less idea what to put in its place. Cromwell himself could only say—and the words are significant of much of his later policy—'I can tell you, Sirs, what I would not have, though I cannot what I would.' Before the Assembly lay approximately three choices: a Puritan State Church, which might or might not retain elements of the older worship with Parliamentary lay Commissioners instead of Bishops ordering its policy; the Presbyterian model; a more or less disestablished Congregationalism. The task of the Scottish Commissioners was to bring the Assembly to accept the second.

The nature and composition of the Assembly made the aims of the Scots far from easy to accomplish. Baillie complained bitterly that it was an Erastian Assembly. It was called by Parliament for purposes laid down by Parliament and forbidden to determine any question other than those laid before it by either or both of the Houses; no foreign correspondence even with the General Assembly could be held without Parliamentary consent, no Assembly production could be published without that consent. Under Scottish promptings, the Assembly became restless under this control, less inclined to be subservient and on occasion openly defiant. Other difficulties lay in the parties formed within the

Assembly and sometimes petty jealousies as well as religious principles divided the members and the Scots had to work as hard at reconciliation as at conversion. The staunch Independents centred round Philip Nye and Thomas Goodwin 'The Five Dissenting Brethren'. As far as there was traditional English Presbyterianism, it was represented by Stephen Marshall and Edmund Calamy. There were others who were really Puritan Anglicans such as Drs Edward Reynolds and John Wallis. There were the Erastians in Dr John Lightfoot and Thomas Coleman. To add to it all, the Scots had the learning of all England arrayed around them; Hebraists such as Lightfoot and Hellenists such as Gattaker, Augustinians such as Twisse, pulpiteers such as Marshall and pamphleteers such as Herle and others as able in all these departments as the men named. They were all Englishmen and scholarly Englishmen; to convert them to Scottish thought was never easy.

The Scots had certain advantages denied to the other members. They were all members of the Grand Committee which was Parliament's agent in dealing with the Assembly. Composed of the Scottish Commissioners, the English Treaty Commissioners and nine members of Assembly, this committee initiated and indicated the matters for debate in the Assembly and revised its final propositions before presenting them to the House. The Scots insisted on being treated as a corporeal and integral part of this Committee without which it could not function, not just as mere individual members. Attempts to oust them from this position failed and they continued to scrutinise the whole transactions from start to finish. They also sat as members of Assembly with full power to debate and were also present in all the three committees into which the Assembly divided itself for discussion and preparation of its various propositions. They had all the advantages of an ever-present, purposeful minority in an intermittent and fluctuating Assembly.

The Assembly had as its President or Prolocutor, Dr William Twisse, the greatest Puritan and Augustinian theologian of his age. He was assisted by Dr Cornelius Burgess and Dr John Whyte as Assessors. Later Charles Herle became Prolocutor, and Herbert

Palmer and, on his death, Dr William Gouge Assessors. The work went on in the way of most Assemblies; free debate was enjoyed on all the set subjects and long speeches endured on many of them. The business was left to twenty or thirty able divines whilst the others attended sporadically and read the news sheets surreptitiously in the back benches. The Assembly met on 1st July 1643. By October and November, the Scots had arrived as the champions of a Presbyterian Britain. The next four chapters will deal with their work without and within the Assembly.

CHAPTER VIII

SCOTTISH ECCLESIASTICAL PROPAGANDA
1641-47

THE ART of political pamphleteering came into effective being during the period of the Civil War. Parties on both sides rapidly learned all the tricks of the trade. Milton, 'Smectymnuus', Hall, Prynne, Edwards were only a few of the multitude whose outpourings found ready sale in the city of London. Dignified pleading, stately prose, violent vituperation and the filthiest of slanderings jostle one another in the pamphlets of the age, often in the pages of the same pamphlet. Since religion and politics were inextricably mixed, pamphleteering on the religious questions of the day was intense and bitter. Prynne had already lost his ears for it, which lent all the more sharpness to his tongue. Bishop Hall and the Smectymnuans had joined issue, with Milton attacking on the flank. John Goodwin, the Ishmael of Coleman Street, was soon shooting arrows in a wide circle at everybody with whom he disagreed and, like Prynne, he soon seemed to disagree with everybody. The Scots were no laggards in the battle. They were well aware that they had to bring not only a section of English divines, but the English people to their own way of thinking. For this, pulpit and pamphlet were the only possible means, and in the City of London where their voice was heard and their pamphlets read, they had a reasonable measure of success; their success in the Assembly was even more outstanding. Indeed they sought city support that they might exert all the more pressure on the Assembly. They came with the powerful backing of the Solemn League and Covenant, but not as blackmailers, rather as missionaries. Few of the Masters, Fellows and Presidents of Colleges or of the English divines of international reputation who assembled were likely to accept even under political pressure anything which their reason disapproved or their scholarship discredited, so the Scots had to convince the best minds in England that the Presbyterian system was workable, enduring—not to say endurable—and warranted by the Word of God. By 1646 they had by debate and propaganda brought the leading Puritan divines of England to regard the Presbyterian system as the proper order of the Church, and had got the London ministers to regard it as *divino jure*. It was the policy of Cromwell and later of Clarendon which prevented Presbyterianism from becoming the established religious order of England.

We saw the ideal of a Presbyterian Britain take shape in the mind of Alexander Henderson during the negotiation of the Treaty of Ripon. He believed, just as Laud did, that the only guarantee of peace between the two kingdoms lay in uniformity of religious persuasion. Elated by their victory over the English army and misled by the anti-prelatic zeal of the English Parliament, the Scots attempted to push on Presbyterian reform before the time was ripe. In a broadsheet of February 1640-41, 'From the Commissioners of Scotland', Henderson overreached himself and one wonders if Gillespie helped him with the vicious attack on Strafford which called for the latter's death with the closing words, 'Better one perish than unity.' He repaired his mistake in a paper entitled 'Our desires concerning unitie in Religion and Uniformitie of Church Government as a special mean to conserve peace in his Majestie's Dominions', which was handed to the English Commissioners for the Treaty on 10th March and temperately stated the Scottish case. 'It is to be wished,' he says, 'that there were one Confession of Faith, one form of Catechism, one Directory for all parts of the public worship of God and prayer, preaching, administration of the Sacraments and one form of Church government in all the Churches of His Majestie's Dominions.' Parliament replied that they were taking into consideration the reformation of Church government and that they would proceed therein in due time 'as shall best conduce to the Glory of God, the peace of the Church and of both Kingdoms'. With this promise and £200,000, the Scots had for the time to be content.

England was at the time awhirl with anti-prelatic pamphleteering and the Scots early and deliberately planned their intervention into this field. As early as October 1640 the Treaty Commissioners at Newcastle sent for Mr Robert Baillie, 'with a number of your *Canterburian's Self Conviction*, together with the warrands thereof and all such papers and proofs as may serve for the purpose'. As they moved south, the scheme widened in scope and deepened in purpose. As was noted in the chapter on Gillespie, an actual propagandist campaign was outlined. Baillie writes that he, Robert Blair and George Gillespie are all to go with Henderson to London, Blair to satisfy the mind of the English Independent, himself to 'convince that prevalent faction against which I have written' and Gillespie 'for the crying down of the English Ceremonies'. The men were well chosen; Blair, reputedly favourable to the evangelical Puritans, was likeliest to win them to a form of Presbyterianism; Baillie, the milder opponent of Episcopacy, was not far from men of Ussher's stamp; Gillespie, resolute opponent of 'Ceremonies', was relied upon to refute all adversaries with the brilliance of his dialectic. Henderson, diplomat more than scholar, drafter of treaties and of laws rather than dialectician, led and tempered the whole team. With the exception of Blair for whom Rutherfurd was substituted, this was later the personnel of the ministerial Westminster Commissioners. Rutherfurd filled the place of Blair because the publication of his *Peacable and Temperate Plea for Paul's Presbyterie* in 1642 made him the acknowledged Scottish authority on the Independent question.

From 1641 onwards these four men, Henderson, Baillie, Gillespie and Rutherfurd, are in the forefront of all ecclesiastical pamphleteering. Even though their works may run to hundreds of pages, the polemic tone is that of the pamphlet. Baillie's *Canterburian's Self Conviction* had appeared in 1640, a general accusation of Anglican Arminianism and Popery. Now in London he followed it up with *A Parallel of the Liturgy and the Mass Book*—a work on much the same lines as his contribution to the original plan. Henderson published anonymously a small tract, *The Unlawfulness and danger of Limited Prelacy* (January 1641). It was a warning from Scots experience that concessions to Charles would be as dangerous in England now as they had been in Scotland in the time of James and it was followed by Baillie's *The Unlawfulness of Limited Episcopacy* in 1641 which enlarged the same theme. To set something more positive before his public, Henderson next published his *Government and Order of the Church of Scotland* (1641). Tactfully written, it claimed that a 'description not a demonstration of the Church of Scotland is intended, *non jus sed factum*, their doing simply and not the reason of their doing'. It was a succinct account of Scottish practice as based on the Books of Discipline and obtruded no divine right though it claimed Scripture warranty. Gillespie's contribution, which has been noted, was the *Assertion of the Government of the Church of Scotland*: it was the argument for the practice outlined in Henderson's *Government and Order* and written without heat but directed against the Anglican position. In this early campaign, Blair seems to have written nothing though Baillie mentions him as having ready a pertinent answer to Bishop Hall's *Remonstrance*, which, if published, has been lost. There was a reason for his silence, stated naïvely by Baillie. 'The English ministers of Holland who are for the New England way are now here. . . . They are all on good terms with us. . . . As for Brownists and Separatists of many kinds, they mislike them as well as we. . . . Our questions with them of the new way we hope to get determined to our mutual satisfaction if we were rid of Bishops; till then we have agreed to speak nothing of anything wherein we differ.' The reason for Blair's silence is manifest in the last sentence. At this time Henderson wrote a Preface to Jeremy Burroughs's—an Independent—*The Petition for Prelates briefly examined*. Policy and a real personal liking for some of these Independents kept the Scots quiet, but, as was noted, when they left England in 1641, they left the English Puritan much to think upon.

The Scots returned to Westminster in 1643 to establish with their English brethren a Church government and worship for both Kingdoms which would be based on the Word of God and the example of the best Reformed Churches and they had little

H

doubt that the best of such examples was to be found in their own worship and practice. They were aware they would have to make some concessions and past experience had shown them the difficulty of their task. Baillie wrote that the people conceived Presbyterianism as a 'strange monster'. It was hydra-headed for the word Presbyterial embraced every shade of opinion from the primitive Episcopal to the near Independent. The reasons for the fixity of the Scottish and the fluidity of the English form of Presbyterianism are obvious. The English form or forms went back through Travers and Cartwright to a more purely Genevan theory—theory rather than model, for Elizabeth and James gave no opportunity for establishing it; the Scottish form was shaped on the model of the French Protestant Church and despite James's Episcopate had had years of national working experience. Cartwright ultimately had to defer to the dictates of the State, and the majority of his followers lived as far as they could in conformity with the Church of England and evaded as far as possible ceremonies abhorrent to their Puritan or Presbyterian principles. The ecclesiastical situation made it impossible for the English Presbyterian to have any 'platform' of Church government and their writers such as Paget merely expounded traditional Genevan theory. Since the time of Andrew Melville, Scotland had a native even if temporarily suppressed Presbyterian system and men, never suppressed, willing to defend it.

It is difficult, therefore, to assess the growth or extent of English Presbyterianism before the date of the Assembly. Dr Shaw believes that the Presbyterianism of Elizabeth's reign and that of Charles's reign were unrelated sporadic outbursts; the first an academic movement, the second an ecclesiastical abortion. M'Crie tries to trace a consistent development in English Presbyterian thought but it would seem that this continuity lies in what Shaw calls the permanent element of English Puritanism rather than in anything definitely Presbyterian. Professor Masson's view is that English Presbyterian principles got buried in the mass of anti-Episcopal polemic and only when Episcopacy was removed were they disinterred. The truth is that in England the

Presbyterian—and the Puritan—was in academic exile—if he held his views too openly, physical exile also was his lot. He was not welcomed at the universities and publication of his views was risky. Dispersion and isolation gave a great variety to Puritan conceptions of Church government in which Presbyterianism shared. It was this amorphous 'Presbyterianism', as much anti-prelatic reaction as anything else, that the Scots sought to mould into obedience to an ideal system.

In those who supported this variety as intrinsic in Church matters and asserted the right of the individual congregation to go its own way, the Scots found their greatest opponents. This Independency was the natural outcome of the Puritan dispersion in Holland, France and New England. A succeeding chapter will deal with the Scottish attitude to the claims for 'separateness' and religious freedom. At the outset the Scots were engaged in winning the majority of anti-prelatic and vaguely Presbyterian divines to their own standpoints in Church government. As they succeeded, their propaganda became less persuasive and more directed towards the complete discrediting of Independency. Such is the power of the interchange of ideas, however, that the Scots were not uninfluenced by Independent thought and in the reverse men like Thomas Goodwin had their Independency characterised by markedly Presbyterian leanings.

The debates in the Assembly which resulted in the completion of the Directory for the Public Worship of God and the Form of Church government were fully supported by a sustained and voluminous controversy outside its doors. In Rutherfurd's *Peacable Plea* (1642), Presbyterianism had been defined with vigour, but without violence against the older Independent school, Ainsworth, Robinson, Johnson, Barrow, Best and the moderate Parker. Now the author had to answer the more militant doctrines of Philip Nye drawn from the practice and precept of the New England divines, expecially of Thomas Hooker and Richard Mather; these were expounded by Thomas Goodwin with capable learning and by John Goodwin with rude vigour. The whole of the contemporary debate on Church government is reflected in Rutherfurd's *The Due Right of Presbyteries, or a Peacable Plea for the Government of the Church of Scotland*. Still comparatively free from rancour, this work is more assertive and provocative than the *Peacable Plea*. After being put to the press, it was more than once stopped while some hastily written 'paper' on the matter of some keen Assembly debate was inserted in the context. Papers on Ruling Elders, Juridical Synods and other themes were pushed in with little regard for the sequence of thought. Despite repetition, bad grammar and strained argument, the *Due Right* is perhaps the most comprehensive apologetic of Scottish Presbyterianism ever written. It was so regarded by the members of Assembly who looked upon it as the Scots' counter-blast to the *Apologetical Narration* of the Independents which had appeared in February 1644 and was a reasoned statement of their case as presented by the 'Five Dissenting Brethren'. More informal exchanges of opinion were held also. The Assembly debates were supplemented by written papers which passed between the contending parties and which were examined and debated in Committee. The 'Brethren' gave their 'Reasons against Certain Propositions concerning Church Government'. The Assembly divines assisted by the Scots answered them. Paper followed paper as the debate wore on and tempers wore out. The whole of this matter was finally collected and published in *The Grand Debate concerning Presbytery and Independency by the Assembly of Divines convened at Westminster by authority of Parliament* (1652).

Henderson's only published contribution to the debate was 'The Reformation of Church Government in Scotland cleared from some Mistakes and Prejudices', issued preparatory to the debate on Presbytery. It is one of his best pamphlets, moderate, reasoned, conciliatory to the former Church of England men whose support he was now going to need. 'We do upon every good reason judge the Church of England in the midst of her "Ceremonies" to have been a true Church and the ministry thereof, notwithstanding the many blemishes and corruptions cleaving unto it, to have been a true ministry and shall never deny unto them that praise whether in debating controversies with

Papists, or in practical divinity for private Christians which they do most justly deserve. Upon the other part we are neither so ignorant nor so arrogant as to ascribe to the Church of Scotland such absolute purity and perfection as hath not need or cannot admit of further Reformation.' So he writes and it is obvious that the Scots are learning to approach their neighbours more tactfully, and even to admire their good works. Happily for him, Gillespie had by now laid off the Ceremonies question and was, as we saw, anonymously laying in to John Goodwin in a preliminary round of the 'toleration' fight. Robert Baillie liked other men to lead off. When the Assembly battle was nearly won, as far as the adoption of a Presbyterian form of government was concerned, he published *An Historicall Vindication of the Government of the Church of Scotland* (1646), a scholarly, readable but not highly original piece of apologetic, owing everything to the men who had spoken before him. He preferred to comment on the *fait accompli* rather than to act as an *agent provocateur*, but his gossip gathering rendered his colleagues many a service. He was their ears, not their tongue.

These were the main publications of the Scots during the debates on Church government and they considerably influenced the mind of the Assembly as seen by the course of the debates and by the ultimate publication of the *Jus Divinum Regiminis Ecclesiastici or the Divine Right of Church Government* by the ministers of the City of London in 1654.

Warned by their experiences in 1641, the Scots published little or nothing in the way of comment on English internal affairs and on the relations between King and Parliament. Political activity was confined to the negotiations of Henderson and the lay Commissioners with Charles at Uxbridge; political comment was confined to their sermons before Parliament. There was one exception—the publication of *Lex Rex* in 1644. Possibly Wariston instigated Rutherfurd to write it at the time of the Uxbridge negotiations. The former never spared an opportunity to humiliate Charles, who disliked him cordially and would dislike more accepting terms from men who sponsored the doctrines of a work in which he was compared to Ahab and his queen to Jezebel. Though the *Lex Rex* was written in reply to the *Sacro-Sanctum Regum Majestas* of John Maxwell, Bishop of Ross—an old foe of Rutherfurd—it was a Scottish intrusion into a pamphlet skirmish of the Civil War. The controversy began with the 'Declaration' of 1642 in which Parliament justified its right to take up arms. The Royalist retort was Dr Ferne's *The Resolving of Conscience* (1642). John Goodwin, Prynne, Herle and others joined in for the Parliament, and Dudley, Diggs, Dr Hammond and John Doughty for the Royalists. Over fifty pamphlets of this controversy exist and doubtless more were written. In *Lex Rex* the right of the subject to resist an unjust Prince and the nature, conditions and duties of a limited monarch are unsparingly laid down. It was twice reissued, in 1648 and in 1657, under different titles when Cromwell and not Charles was Instans Tyrannus.

Two other fields of Scottish religious controversy remain. One, the Erastian controversy, has been outlined in the chapter on George Gillespie. The other was the 'Toleration' question which revealed the confused arena in which the Scots were fighting, showed some justification in the demands for order, and elicited a dogmatic attitude to religions other than their own. It is worth a small chapter to itself.

Let us turn back for a minute to the Erastian affair. With few exceptions, all the members of the Assembly believed that the Church through her ministers had the right to exclude unworthy members from the Sacraments and with a few exceptions all the members of Parliament were determined to restrain the divines from framing propositions which would put into practice an authoritarian Church dogma of Excommunication and censure. Parliament's supporters in the Assembly were Coleman and Lightfoot, the Hebraists who drew their main arguments from the 'Thesis' of Erastus and its 'Vindication' which was concerned primarily with the matter of excommunication and the limitation of its use. The excommunication debates inevitably projected a clash between Assembly and Parliament over the measure of control the State could exercise over the Church and over the freedom from interference which the latter should enjoy. Because of the original cause of the conflict—excommunication—and because of the apologetic use of Erastus' works by Parliament's penmen, those who supported State control of the Church came to be called 'Erastians'. George Gillespie damned them with that name and gave the word to the English language though the doctrines of Coleman, Selden and Prynne would not have been altogether acceptable to Erastus himself.

As we saw in our study of Gillespie, the Assembly debates on Excommunication were tempestuous and turbulent. The 'Humble Advice' regarding suspension from the Sacrament of the Lord's Supper, and the Directory for Excommunication which the divines presented to Parliament early in 1645 were rejected. The Commons claimed the right to prescribe the sins which rendered suspension justifiable and asserted the right of Parliament to hear pleas against any such suspension. Coleman preached his famous sermon and Gillespie began the attack. The Assembly petitioned Parliament in August claiming *jure divino* the Church's age-old right to suspend from the Sacrament and asserted that the State had no right in this matter. Minor concessions were granted but the divines, having caught some of Gillespie's spirit, refused to be content with these and pressed for a fuller satisfaction further than Baillie, always timid, considered safe, and Henderson, always politic, considered wise. The Assembly was publicly rebuked by the House and their 'advice' voted a breach of privilege. The right to control excommunication was never surrendered by the English civil power; the list of censurable offences was enlarged, but appeal was still allowed and provincial civil commissioners were appointed to try cases not in the categories. The debate became a matter of high policy, for the Assembly was at the same time debating chapter XXX of the Confession: 'That Jesus Christ as King and Head of the Church has appointed an ecclesiastical government in His Church in the hand of Church officers distinct from civil government.' The passing of this proposition was a crowning triumph for the Scots.

Even the Independents had to vote against the Erastians for not even for the sake of a political alliance with the State could they forswear their essential principles of religious freedom, though astutely they kept out of the pamphleteering arena.

The great protagonists in the conflict were, for the divines, the Scots and the ministers of London, for the 'Erastians', Coleman, Selden, Prynne and Lightfoot. The anonymous pamphlet *A Late Dialogue betwixt a civilian and a divine concerning the present condition of the Church of England*, if it is Gillespie's, was the opening attempt to spring the Erastian hares from their ecclesiastical coverts. When they arose, not to flee but to fight, the bitterest and the most vindictive of the Assembly's paper wars began. The opening charge came from Rutherfurd with the publication of his *The Divine Right of Church Government and Excommunication*. It was written during the winter of 1645-46 under pressure which nearly broke his health and was intended to forestall Coleman who was reputed to be bringing out an edition of Erastus. The *Divine Right* attempted to answer everything the Erastians had said or were going to say, in 750 quarto pages. The intellectual Erastianism of Hooker, the ecclesiastical Erastianism of Erastus, the political Erastianism of Prynne, were tenaciously and tediously connoted, confuted and condemned, along with the semi-Erastian principles of the Aberdeen Doctors whipped in for good measure. Passages from the daily arguments of the Assembly were rammed into the conglomeration. Rutherfurd was aware of the hasty 'get up' of the book for in his preface he says, 'Others can and I hope will add riper animadversions to Erastus.' He referred to Gillespie, at present hot in conflict with Coleman but also at work on his *magnum opus, Aaron's Rod Blossoming* (1646), which, when it appeared, was the most orderly, historic and lucid examination and confutation of Erastian principles which the Assembly produced. An account of his part in this affair has already been given. He added at the end of his stay the *CXI Propositions* also already mentioned.

Gillespie and Rutherfurd certainly converted the ministers of London to a completely anti-Erastian conception of Church policy for their *Jus Divinum Regiminis Ecclesiastici* (1646 and in three subsequent editions) asserts dogmatically everything that they had been teaching and preaching in the last two years and much that the English Presbyterian had never dared to claim. Bitter though the conflict was and mistaken though the Scots and divines might be in some of their supporting contentions, they were absolutely right in their assertion of the spiritual freedom of the Church. When they come to consider the religious freedom of the individual they show up—according to modern conceptions—in a much less favourable light. Yet even in the Toleration controversy, there is something to be said for their point of view at the time, even if its merit is concealed in a welter of ecclesiastical invective and scurrilous abuse.

CHAPTER IX

THE TOLERATION CONTROVERSY

IT HAD been claimed by historians such as Dr Shaw that Presbyterianism lost the day in England because men's hearts were with
the old order and the Prayer Book, and that a slow passive resentment at Presbyterianism increasingly grew in the ordinary
Englishman with every action of the Scots, so that at the Restoration they turned with gladness to the old Anglican order. This is
only half a truth, barely a half truth. Certainly if the Presbyterians
had allowed the Prayer Book to be retained in England, as earlier,
if Laud had kept the same book out of Scotland, the ecclesiastical
state of each country might have borne a different aspect. The
Prayer Book was dear to many Englishmen, but how dear and to
how many is difficult to ascertain, for not every Royalist was a
Hyde or a Falkland. The more potent foe of Presbyterianism—
and of Episcopacy—was the spirit of individualism, and of
eccentric individualism, working even more in religious than in
political affairs, where vested interests of land and trade still kept
undue aberrations curbed and circumscribed—all the more so as
this spirit found expression in the multifarious sects, creeds, fan-
tasies and fanaticisms of the age. How numerous and how
eccentric these were is difficult to judge, so distorted and exploited
were they by Presbyterian propaganda. Some deviations from
orthodox Calvinism were slight and some of the hated Anabaptists were Calvinist in all but the Baptist principle; others, like
the maunderings of the poor half-wit—or humorist in bad taste—
who said that 'the Earl of Essex made him, Sir William Waller
redeemed him, and the Earl of Manchester sanctified him', manifested a diseased brain rather than a distorted theology. All were
treated with a grim and humourless severity. Petitions to Parliament against heresy and even individual heretics were sent up

from the Assembly. It became part of the Presbyterian policy to set forth every ludicrous, revolting or contentious eccentricity which came to light as an argument against Independency and the chaos to which it would lead.

Allowing for exaggeration, misrepresentation and invective, the years of the Civil War and the Protectorate saw a huge increase in the number of sects, decorous and otherwise, which infuriated the orthodox and enlivened local politics in town and country. Edwards in his 'Antapologia' to the *Apologetical Narration* of the Independents, writes of 'swarms and troops of Independents'. Baxter speaks of Independency, Anabaptistry, Antinomianism and Arminianism, and combinations and permutations of them all as being rife in Cromwell's army. From the *Gangraena* of Thomas Edwards and the *Dissuasive from the Errors of the Time* of Robert Baillie a catalogue of every known—and unknown—heresy, great or small, existing between 1600 and 1650 could be made. Chief among these were the Baptists, called Anabaptists to damn them with the reproach of Munster. There were, by 1646, fifty-four Baptist churches, seven in London, and the rapid growth of this sect may have been responsible for much of the obscene vituperation they endured. The Old Brownists were the extreme Independents with out-and-out toleration claims. Antinomianism was by now a personal creed rather than a religious sect, but anyone, anything and everything that was anti-Calvinist and could not be otherwise classified, was labelled Antinomian by Edwards. The Familists' peculiarities are difficult to discover, but under the heading seem to come the quietists, pantheists, mystics or pseudo-mystics of the time. Millenaries and Chiliasts, decent and extravagant, had their place. The Seekers were blind to the glory of Presbyterianism, Episcopacy and Independency, and still sought the true Church. Divorcers, like John Milton, anti-Sabbatarians, like poor John Trask, Soulsleepers, Arians, Socinians, anti-Trinitarians, made up the number. In the *Gangraena* is a collection of 176 errors, heresies and blasphemies. The author simply collected and adumbrated every heresy, ancient and modern, which he knew, and attributed them to the sects in

England. The more violent a heresy, the more useful was it as propaganda. Arianism, Socinianism, and their dependent dogmas are all included, as are Arminianism, Amyraldism, and every other anathema to the Calvinist. The thoughts of religious genius, the ironies of an opponent taken seriously, the dreams of the mystic, the haverings of the village idiot, are all jumbled together as alike heretical and damnable. Edwards has no sense of proportion, and consequently none of humour. 'A fluent, rancorous, indefatigable, inquisitorial and on the whole nasty kind of Christian'—the words are Professor Masson's—it is a pity that some of the Scots followed in his literary footsteps. The latter were honestly revolted by the stupidity, indecency and sheer wildness of mental deficiency which brought forth queer fruit in many of the sects and an ordered, established and disciplinary Presbyterian Church was their panacea.

As the number of sects and opinions grew, so the demand for Toleration increased. Some were prepared enough to accept Toleration for themselves and deny it to others, for example, the moderate Independents, in self defence, were only moderate Tolerationists. The more extreme and extravagant the opinion, as a rule, the more acute was the demand for unlimited Toleration. On the whole, the sects, differing in all else, were united in their demand for Toleration and were Independent in that they were self-supporting and desirous of a self-controlled existence. The Presbyterian had thus a facile case for making Independency the root of all evil, though the real Independents had nothing in common with the religious fantastics. Toleration of religious difference was an abomination to Presbyterian, Romanist and Anglican because it was destructive of the keystones in their respective ecclesiastical structures, the infallible Word, the inerrant Church, or the omnipotent State. Each Church had vigorous arguments against the practice, often very similar in nature and content and Rutherfurd will be found citing, with commendation, Jesuit lawyers to support his case. Of all these Churches, only in the Anglican, among the Cambridge Platonists, was an approach to a limited idea of Toleration made.

Few supported absolute Toleration, for there were extravagances which no Church, State or sectary could countenance. The more moderate of the last were willing to make scapegoats of the extremists to testify to their own righteousness and win toleration and a certain amount of establishment for themselves. The Independents howled as loud as any for Paul Best's blood. The truest sponsors of Toleration were the Baptists, its happiest exponent Roger Williams, founder of Rhode Island Colony with its laws of universal suffrage and liberty of conscience. While in England, Williams published *The Bloody Tenet of Persecution for Cause of Conscience discussed in a Conference between Truth and Peace*, wisely enough after his negotiations with Parliament for the status of his colony had been completed, for he advocated the absolute toleration of all sect, error or atheism and the complete disestablishment of religion, even maintaining that neither error nor heresy need debar a man from holding high office in the State. His Independent brethren in England and New England shuddered in his company and were glad when he removed the reproach from them by becoming a Baptist. Henry Burton, the Independent Martyr, and John Goodwin, the Colossus of Coleman Street, were practically absolute Tolerationists. They fell short of Williams in holding that Congregational Churches had the power to deal with error in their midst, even to excommunication, and they allowed the State to encourage ministers in the confutation and elimination of heresy, barring always the application of any physical, legal or social sanctions. Whilst disliking a national Church, they tolerated it.

The most dangerous to the Scots was the limited Toleration claimed by Nye and the dissenting Brethren. The claims of Williams were equally repellent to Church and State, those of Burton and Goodwin hardly less so, for any concessions they made were so patently sprats to catch Leviathan that there was little likelihood of that monster swallowing them. But the brethren plausibly asked for toleration of congregational practices by the established Church—presumed to be Presbyterian—and relief of the more godly of the sects from persecution and boycott. They excluded from such relief Episcopalians, Antinomians, Arians and all holders of glaring heresies. It is difficult to discern what was their ultimate ecclesiastical policy and object. Often at Westminster their attitude seems purely and simply 'dog in the manger', and Nye, the opportunist, tied his party so tightly to Cromwell's chariot wheels that their policy became identical with the Army's. They might have welcomed an established Independency such as existed in New England, where the government granted great powers of discipline and wide privileges to the local Congregational Churches, although not endowing them. As Nye had no scruples in accepting revenues from Kimbolton, his policy may have visualised New England Congregationalism plus endowment. (It may be said here that New England Congregationalism was no more tolerant than Scottish Presbyterianism.) To secure the toleration at which they aimed, the Independents, in 1644, had to widen their claims to gain Army support although they still anathematised flagrant heresy. The establishment of Presbyterianism with freedom of worship for all decent men who differ was implied in the Heads of the Proposals of August 1647, but in October the Agreement of the People first claimed 'absolute freedom on the matter of Religion and the ways of God's Worship', then grudgingly conceded that the State might set up 'some public way of instructing the nation so it be not compulsive'. The rake's progress of Independency, which the Scots had feared, was almost accomplished; it was fulfilled and crowned in the Cromwellian regime. Meanwhile the aim and policy of the Scots and their Presbyterian allies was, as described by Professor Masson, 'to tie Toleration round the neck of the Independents, stuff the two struggling monsters into one sack and sink them in the bottom of the sea'.

Was this policy sound? The same historian writes, 'They [the Scots] stood stoutly to the necessary identity of Presbyterianism and absolute anti-Toleration and so Presbyterianism missed the most magnificent opportunity she has had in her history.' Perhaps! but if the Scots were dour, the Independents were thrawn. A little less truculence, a little more compromise, when the Scots were at the zenith of their power might have won the Independents to live peaceably with the Presbyterian regime. As passions died, they would have merged with the larger body. If both parties had made some compromise on the Prayer Book and accepted the moderate Episcopalian into fellowship, the Church of England might have been far greater in number, wider in outlook and happier in relation to her neighbours than her story reveals. On the other hand, the reforming spirit and evangelistic zeal begotten in the Free Churches of that nation would have suffered great loss. As it was, Nye would certainly have taken offered compromise as a sign of weakness, and the Scots had no guarantee that the Independents, once satisfied, would remain satisfied. In town and country they waged a persistent guerilla warfare, and so the Scots decided to fight it out with their opponents on the complete anti-Toleration platform, mercilessly attacking pretended liberty of conscience, scorning few opportunities to smirch and befoul the Independent nest and its brood.

There is again evidence of a Scottish propagandist plan, Baillie and Rutherfurd being now its agents. Their productions in relation to this controversy were: Baillie's *Dissuasive from the Errors of the Time* (1645) and his *Anabaptism the true Fountain of Independency, Antinomy, Brownism and Familism* (1647), and Rutherfurd's *Survey of the Spiritual Anti-Christ* (1648) and his *Free Disputation against Pretended Liberty of Conscience* (1649). The first of Rutherfurd's works was given to the printer before he left London in November 1647 and published early in 1648; the last was a summary of the experience of the Scottish Westminster Commissioners between 1644 and 1647. Baillie's *Dissuasive* was partly a popular counterpart of Rutherfurd's and Gillespie's works on Independency. Erudite and learned himself, he had a more fluent pen than his colleagues and, like Mr Edwards, a 'penchant' for collecting gossip, so his work was more akin to the 'Antapologia' of the latter and he was not above plagiarism of some of its matter. Baillie's arguments were historical and pragmatic, or apparently so. He demonstrated that Independency had a bad spiritual ancestry and was begetting a worse progeny;

outlining the rise and progress of Brownism at home, in Holland and in New England, he inserted for illustration all the stock scandals connected with the more fantastic elements. Though not so scurrilous as Edwards, he obviously enjoyed the narration of a scandal whilst protesting that he told it reluctantly.

But the Five Dissenting Brethren were able to withstand the onslaught, and though the Presbyterians had outed John Goodwin from Coleman Street, they could not silence his pen. The sins of Brownism tied as a millstone round the neck of Independency had not sufficed to sink the monster, so a heavier load had to be found. Of course the indefatigable Mr Edwards found it. The Baptist faith had gained ground. Why it was selected for so bitter an attack, is difficult nowadays to understand, for some of the Baptists were Calvinist in all but the doctrine of paedo-baptism though Helwisse, the founder of the first Baptist Church in London, was an Arminian; German Anabaptism was in some ways a nasty ancestor; the doctrine of complete immersion—enemies said naked immersion—led to some gross stories of queer practices, ill-founded and probably rare; but in fact the English Baptists leapt into ill-repute, till the queer Quakers came to take their place, because they were a very convenient whip with which to scourge the Independent. Ostracised by Lutheran and Calvinist, they were, of course, Independents in their conception of Church government, and Edwards could scream at the increase in Baptists as the evil fruit of Independency and Toleration. He did this in his *Gangraena, or a Catalogue and Discovery of many of the Errors, Heresies, Blasphemies and pernicious Practices of the Sectaries of this time vented and acted in England in the last four years* (1645-46). It was enlarged in a later edition. Great play was made with stories of baptism of naked women. He sent out for and invited such stories; some as to how, why and where Independent and Baptist pastors got their money were dirty insinuations or wilful misrepresentations of the principle of voluntaryism; others relate the acts of the mentally deranged or the religiously eccentric, or merely practices not conforming to Presbyterianism. Baillie unfortunately followed Edwards in his *Anabaptism the True*

Fountain of Independency. The title was a plain statement of the Presbyterian policy of collecting millstones. He was more scholarly and lucid and selective than Edwards; the method and the intent to procure repressive action through slanderous vilification was the same. Much of the matter comes from Edwards, cleansed somewhat, but there was a rather ill-concealed glee at being able to hint at gross obscenities.

The Independent monster still refused to drown, rather swam the more steadily with the current of military favour. By 1647 the sects calling themselves Independent had multiplied; the measures of Toleration claimed by the Army in its negotiations with Charles, now in its power, encouraged bold statement of belief—or disbelief—in pulpit and pamphlet. Rutherfurd had been left alone in 1647 to fight a rearguard action. He took up his pen reluctantly to write *A Survey of the Spiritual Anti-Christ, opening the Secrets of Familism and Antinomianism.* This from the Scottish side was the final dragnet; every obscure heresy that had escaped notice could be crushed into these two categories. Mysticism, anti-Trinitarian heresy, Pantheism, were charged against the Antinomians and the reproach of David George and Caspar Schwenkfeld laid upon them. Every hidden and suspected lewdness and monstrosity were popularly attributed to 'Familism'. Who and what the Familists were is difficult to ascertain, even from this reputed work on the subject; mystics such as Peter Sterry were included in their number as also was John Saltmarsh —no mystic, but a Cromwellian pamphleteer dabbling in mysticism.

When Toleration became Army dogma, Independency with its variations and aberrations was safe from politician and pamphleteer. As the shadows lengthened in the unhappy years of the Engagement, Rutherfurd saw the apparently fatal disease of Toleration destroying orderly religious life in England and threatening Scotland itself. Late in 1647, Edwards the irrepressible had published *The Casting Down of the Last Stronghold of Satan or A Treatise against Toleration and Pretended Liberty of Conscience.* In 1649—written throughout 1648—Rutherfurd published *A Free*

I

Disputation against Pretended Liberty of Conscience as the Scottish contribution. A study of this work will show the whole Presbyterian doctrine that lay behind the bitter pamphleteering attack on the Independents.

Edwards had been content with a fluent Old Testament justification of religious suppression as his main argument. Rutherfurd went deeper. He expounded Calvin's definition of conscience as 'a sense of divine justice' so as to remove any remote connection with a doctrine of the Inner Light. Accordingly, for him, conscience was a power of the practical understanding by which man was obliged to give judgement of himself, of his state and condition and all his actions, inclinations, thoughts and words. It could thus be disciplined and informed and was not a supremely free agent dictating a man's religious beliefs, but subject to the proper inculcation of the Word of God, and it was the duty of Church and State to correct the errant conscience. This was Roman dogma which hardly went underground till it became a *sine qua non* of the Reformers and we find Rutherfurd quoting Jesuit jurists in support of his argument.

For the Presbyterian, the agents of this correction were the 'Synods' of the Church who interpreted the Word of God for its members, but Protestant hesitancy to declare synods infallible placed him in a quandary, for how could a synod composed of fallible men infallibly correct error in other men? The Scots came near to asserting a doctrine of synodical infallibility. It was no answer to this charge for them to say that when the synod commanded anything contrary to the Word of God, men need not obey, for the question still remained—who is to judge what is contrary? The later Calvinist passed quietly over the doctrine of the priesthood of all believers because the Arminian, applying it to the doctrine of the sufficiency of Scripture, formed the doctrine of the right of individual interpretation of Scriptures. To counter this claim, Rutherfurd and the later Calvinists asserted the right of the Church synod alone authoritatively to interpret the Word in fundamentals of faith.

The magistrate had a duty to help the Church in the elimination of error; he did not compel or convert a subject into the true faith, but he was a trustee for it, who, by extirpating false beliefs created the healthy atmosphere in which true religion would flourish. This is pure Bellarmine from the Protestant and Presbyterian angle. Thus the argument proceeds and the planned Confession of Faith becomes less a Confession and more and more a touchstone to search out and wither the evils of heresy. An elaborate sieve of fundamentals, super-fundamentals and circa-fundamentals and praeter-fundamentals is created to winnow out Presbyterian wheat from alien chaff and to aid the Church courts and officiating magistrates in their task. Rutherfurd can even write, 'Errors in non-fundamentals obstinately held are punishable.'

Such a doctrine of non-toleration demanded the pursuit of a supporting policy. Schismatic and heretic were to be silenced. None was to be allowed to preach according to the dictates of an 'inner light'. The death penalty was the judgement for the obstinate heretic. A good deal of this bloodthirstiness was theoretic and due to the excessive use of Old Testament analogy for, even in the very heat of his argument, Rutherfurd can say, 'We are not obliged by Scripture to kill every ignorant, blinded Papist with the sword.' It is specifically stated that no nation can be converted by the power of the sword but only by missionary effort. Jews, for example, were not to be persecuted but instructed. But a nation which had sworn to establish the true religion in alliance with a neighbour and had broken her oath could be compelled to keep her bargain. This was the England of 1647 in the grip of Cromwell which did not implement the Solemn League and Covenant although the Westminster standards of religious uniformity were now in Parliament's hands. Rutherfurd's last doctrine is doubtless very reprehensible but it seems still the practice to reimpose the conditions of a broken treaty on the offender by economic, political and military sanctions, if the offended has the power to make these effective.

Although Rutherfurd will always be classed as an anti-Erastian, in the *Due Right* he had stated that the Magistrate had a directly spiritual end, which statement he qualified in the *Divine Right*, when face to face with the Erastian Parliament. The *Free Dispensation* was in some respects a return to his first position, for the suppression of heresy and the preservation of truth were directly religious ends. It must be admitted that an Independent suffering at the hands of a Presbyterian magistrate what seemed an intolerable interference with his religious practice, could not but view the Presbyterian as Erastian. It is easy to write harshly when reading the bitter utterances of these intolerant men and to feel that the finer word was Jeremy Taylor's when he wrote, 'He who persecutes a heretic arms the world against himself,' though the Anglican in power paid little heed to the *Liberty of Prophesying*. On the other hand, Froude has written, 'You cannot tolerate what will not tolerate you and is trying to cut your throat.' The Scottish policy of anti-Toleration was a measure of self defence, although a mistaken and a violent one. But the same problem is still with us. Face to face with Communism, we are reminded that the problems of toleration are eternal, that the power of the magistrate can still be invoked to suppress an alien or subversive creed, that in home or foreign affairs little scruple is shown in following Rutherfurd's dogmas when a national crisis arises.

Such were the propagandist labours of the Scots, enhanced by their personal contacts. There was, in the early years, more harmony among the divines than all this controversy suggests. The Scots debated with the Independents but they dined with them very pleasantly. There were many circles in which each found his own niche, a friendly social life, even to intermarriage between families, existed among the members of the Assembly. Friendships made outside the House meant allies within it and Henderson and his compatriots were alive to this all the time of their stay at Westminster. Much more may have been achieved through their personal contacts than appears in the actual debates. Finally, for popular appeal they depended on the pulpit, for all of them were preachers, and two of them among the best of their time—or of any time.

Henderson preached less frequently now. He was tied to the task of negotiating and ill-health was a heavy burden. Baillie loved the limelight—when it was safe to stand in it. He was a fluent, rather featureless preacher saying little that would offend, or what would offend only the minority, and saying it fairly well. Gillespie and Rutherfurd drew the crowd and cared little whom they offended. The last Wednesday of each month was an appointed Fast Day, when a sermon was preached before the Commons in St. Margaret's, generally by one of the Assembly divines and frequently also one was preached before the Lords in the Abbey. These sermons are invaluable revelations of the ecclesiastical reaction to the crisis of the hour. This Fast Day was quite an occasion for the preacher—and Parliament—theatres being at a discount. The preachers indeed complained that these days were feasts rather than fasts; Whincop upbraided his listeners for their sumptuous apparel and low-cut gowns in none too delicate a manner.

The Scottish contributions to the Westminster sermons are of great interest if only to show the great freedom which they were still allowed in dealing with English affairs. They all preached a sermon before Lords and before Commons. Henderson preached also on 18th July 1644, at the Thanksgiving for Marston Moor; the rest of the Scottish sermons were centred on the Erastian controversy. Henderson again preached, reluctantly, on 28th May 1645. Using the text, 'My Kingdom is not of this world', in his plain, forthright style, he warned Parliament to beware of lukewarmness, divisions and delays. In June, Rutherfurd preached on 'The Calming of the Tempest' with at one and the same time the bite of a Gillespie and the almost macabre sonority of a Donne, and yet with an inward yearning for peace that was peculiarly his own. The great occasion moved him to think of the transiency of human greatness. 'It were a right timing of actions if the honourable Parliament would begin not at the building or the establishing of their own Liberties, Laws, Houses, but at the building of the House of God.' Looking down on his privilege-proud audience, he goes on, 'Within a few generations, there shall be a Parliament of other faces, a new generation of other men in the Cities, Houses, Assemblies we are now in, and we, a company of night visions shall fly away and our place shall know us no more. . . . What poor thoughts we shall have of this poor ball of clay, this earth, when the worms shall creep in through face and cheek . . . or imagine our spirits once entered within the line of eternity could but stay up beside the moon and look down and behold us children sweating and running for our beloved shadows of Lands, Flocks, Castles, Towers, Crowns, Sceptres, Gold, Money; they should wonder that reason is so blear-eyed as to hunt dreams and toys.' He damned war profiteers in one sentence: 'These that would draw to themselves gain from the public now would crucify Christ for his coat.' In a fine passage, he is a good deal more Christian than his controversy. 'Shall we kill and devour one another all day and lodge together in heaven at night and can we say to one another in heaven "Hast thou found me, Oh mine enemy?" Shall there be any factions, any sides, either religions of Presbyterian and Independent in heaven or nations of England and Scotland (which differ not essentially (I am sure) except in the poor accidents of North and South) and yet in earth we must be at daggers, at rentings, at divisions; are there two Christs because two nations?' How often all parties were to forget these truths in the following days and years.

Baillie's sermon before the Lords, on 30th July, was of a different nature. He complimented them for suppressing Mr Archer's heretical book, perhaps to neutralise the acid of Rutherfurd's indictment, and taking the text, 'Lord, why hast thou made us to err from Thy ways?' (Isa. 63.7), preached a fluent and sincere sermon on sin, especially the sins of the Malignants, Independents and Antinomians. The Lords doubtless dismissed to add a heresy or two to Parliament's list in reward for worthy Mr Baillie's sermon. Gillespie found this sort of preaching little to his liking and when his turn came, preached the sermon, from Mal. 3.2, 'Who shall abide the day of his coming?', which set the whole Erastian controversy ablaze. 'No effectual reformation can be looked for till rulers and magistrates be reformed', he told them with passionate directness.

Thus, outside the Assembly doors, the Scots sought and used every opportunity to make their voice heard and their cause known. We can now watch their success in the Assembly itself.

CHAPTER X

WESTMINSTER AND CHURCH GOVERNMENT

THE NATURAL RESULT of the Solemn League and Covenant was to make the determination of a 'Form of Church Government' the first concern of the Assembly and to drop, for the time being, the more purely doctrinal matters under consideration. The descent of the Scots upon the Assembly was the impact of a small body of men, with knowledge of a practical model which they had developed, upon a heterogeneous conference whose knowledge of Presbyterianism was theoretical and traditional. They had the great advantage of knowing what they wanted.

When debates started, certain doctrines held in common caused little argument. Parliament's abolition of the hierarchy made parity of the clergy an accepted and acceptable dogma and the nature of the pastor's office was something upon which all agreed. Preaching, ruling, administering the Sacraments, catechising, visiting the sick, were all accepted as pertaining to his office as was also reading of the Scriptures. Over this last, there was minor disagreement. Some of the Englishmen, in particular the Smectymnuans, were inclined to hold that the Reader was a distinct office. The Scots affirmed that this office had in Scotland only been regarded as temporary. 'We acknowledge no reading pastors but only pastors gifted, who are able to cut the Word aright', states Rutherfurd in his *Peacable Plea*; and so the office of Reader was expunged from the Form of Church Government. Another difference arose during discussion of the 'Doctor's' office which raised the question as to whether a minister could be ordained without a charge. The Independents held that the pastor and teacher were distinct offices in substance and one of each should be placed in every congregation. The less extreme Puritans

believed that a man could be ordained without a charge and that
such a man of brilliant parts might, as Fellow of a College, be a
'Doctor' there; but the distinction was in gifts, not office. The
Scottish view lay somewhere between these: the doctor differed
in name and function from the pastor; he was an elder *ex officio*,
with power in Kirk Courts but with no right to administer the
Sacraments unless called thereto. There seems to have been in
Henderson and Rutherfurd's time a tendency to degrade the
rank of 'Doctor' from his original status in the Book of Discipline,
for, at the beginning of this debate, they are found arguing that
it is only expedient that the Doctor hold the Elder's office. As
the debate proceeded, they reverted to the older Scottish position
and also conceded the Doctor's right to administer the Sacraments. A proposition was framed which suited all parties. 'The
Scripture doth hold out the name and title of teacher as well as
pastor, who also is a minister of the Word as well as the pastor
and hath power of administration of the Sacrament.' Later was
added, 'A teacher or doctor is of most excellent use in schools
and colleges.' Since this time, many branches of the Presbyterian
Church have insisted on their professors being ordained ministers.

Over the office of Elder the debate was keen. Such an office
was almost unknown to the present generation of English pastors
who conceived a Presbytery or classis to be an authoritative
meeting of ministers and a Kirk Session as a consultative meeting
of the minister with minor lay officials. It took hard pressure
from the Scots and from the Independents who were equally
assertive of the elder's office to bring the majority of the English
clergy to acknowledge it as scripturally warranted. Basing their
arguments on 1 Tim. 5.17, Scots and Independents argued that
there were two kinds of Presbyters, those who rule and those who
labour in the Word and Doctrine. The majority maintained that
the text referred to gift and talent, not to office. The English
cleric was as distrustful of a lay element in ecclesiastical office as
Henderson and the Scots were convinced of its necessity, or
rather of the necessity of elders, for they avoided calling their
elders laymen. It would be incorrect, however, to make the

latter subscribe completely to the 'presbyter' doctrine of the eldership held in some branches of the Presbyterian Church. The Englishman placed a sacramental value on ordination and conceived it as in some way conveying the apostolic succession. In this case, the Scots remembered the doctrine of the priesthood of all believers and held ordination to be simply the orderly setting apart of a man to office in the sight of God in which they were supported by the Independents, though they came to differ fiercely from them over the question of the ordainers. After much debate the final proposition emerged as: 'As there were in the Jewish Church elders of the people . . . So Christ who hath instituted a Government and Governors ecclesiastical in the Church, hath furnished some in His Church beside the ministers of the Word with gifts for Government and with commission to execute the same when called thereunto; who are to join with the minister in the Government of the Church (Rom. 12.7-8, 1 Cor. 12.28) which officers, Reformed Churches commonly call elders. 1 Tim. 5.17 was never accepted as a proof text, but as far as Presbyterianism became practised in England, the name 'elder' became current for 'other Church Governors'.

What is the elder—cleric or layman? The Second Book of Discipline states that the eldership is a spiritual function as is the ministry, but no conclusive argument for the 'lay' or 'presbyter' theory can be built on this. As noted, because of adherence to the 'priesthood of all believers', distinction between 'lay' and 'presbyter' was less clear-cut among the Scots and Independents than among the rest of the native English clergy. To establish the office of elder, the Scots stated a higher doctrine than in practice they followed. They claimed a ruling eldership *divino jure*, but the authoritative preaching of the Word and the administration of the Sacraments was retained to the ministry. For this they claimed 1 Tim. 5.17 as warrant but in effect they made the elder of lesser rank and ordination. The doctrine of the eldership, as defined at Westminster, was like many another doctrine, historically conditioned. Still, the success of the Scottish argument can be measured by the fact that when later in 1647, during the

Erastian debate, it was proposed that 'the government which is *divino jure* is that which is by preaching and ruling elders in Presbyteries and Synods by way of subordination and appeal', the supporters of the proposition included Gouge, Burgess, Marshall, Calamy, Young, Ashe and many others who had originally opposed the introduction of the office of the ruling elder; this too at a time when Scottish political influence was waning.

The office of Deacon was accepted with little or no debate. So far, the Scots and Independents had been in alliance, almost in amity and Rutherfurd and Baillie write pleasantly of their relationship. Now, when the Assembly went on to consider the nature of government by Church Courts, the violence of the debate rent them finally apart. The alliances change. The Scots and the majority of the English divines were all products of a national Church, albeit of different traditions. They united in opposing the creation and indeed the existence of an Independent Church order seemingly utterly subversive of a national system. The Independents' 'desires' were completely alien alike to those brought up in a Presbyterian and an Episcopalian Church. When the proposition, 'The Scripture holdeth forth that many congregations may be under one Presbyterian Government', came before the Assembly, the battle began between Scot and Independent which was to issue into a violent pamphlet contest and end in national strife. The debates were lengthy, syllogistic and polemical, their burden inside and outside the Assembly falling on Rutherfurd and Gillespie.

The Independents maintained the 'separateness' of each congregation and held that a Presbytery could only be a fraternal consultative body without jurisdictive power. The Scots insisted on the power and jurisdiction of the Presbytery as a Court of the Church. Varieties of opinion existed among the others; some were not inclined to allow elders into the Presbyterial court; others were dubious of the power of excommunication to be vested in it, which the Independents claimed belonged only to the congregation or to the congregation in its officers. There was a surprising variety of doctrine within these narrow limits. During the debate, the Independents penned their famous *Apologetic Narration* protesting against the Presbyterial system of Church government and claiming the right to order churches in their own way. Nye, when he had a 'gallery' of House of Commons men, viciously attacked Presbyterianism as incompatible with civil government. Cromwell attempted to have the debates shelved. Despite delay, intrigue and manoeuvre, the Scots doggedly fought the issue to a successful conclusion. They prevailed on the Assembly to accept exegetical proofs for 'Presbytery' which now appear less sound than their Timothy proof for the eldership.

For a moment, when the Assembly considered the power of congregations and Kirk Sessions, the Scots and Independents came a little nearer. Rutherfurd, who later was instrumental in Scotland in making the popular election of ministers the law of the Kirk, now stood out for the rights of the congregation and Nye claimed him as approaching very nearly to the Independents' point of view, but others still regarded the elder's office with apprehension and maintained that one elder in a congregation was sufficient, distrusting the power they might gain collectively in a 'congregational assembly'. The Scots won the day for it was finally determined: 'For officers in a single congregation there ought to be one at least both to labour in the Word and doctrine and to rule. It is also requisite that there should be others to join in government. The number . . . of which is to be proportioned according to the condition of the congregation.' To the 'Congregational Assembly' (Kirk Session) was given power of discipline and of suspending from the Lord's Table. The Independents were prepared to give these powers to the 'Congregational Assembly' but to no other. It may be noted that, hitherto in Scotland, the Kirk Session had been, according to Calderwood, considered more as a sub-committee of Presbytery. Its establishment as a separate juridical court owed something to Scottish contact with Independent thought at Westminster. Rutherfurd's views on the election of ministers were certainly confirmed by similar contact.

When the Assembly went back to consider the four-fold assemblies of the Church, congregational, classical, provincial and national, animosity between Scot and Independent was kindled afresh; the system of Church courts and of appeal upwards through them was bitterly debated. The need of Scottish military support, owing to the defeat of Essex, gave Henderson a strong political hold and in the teeth of Independent opposition all the important propositions establishing the Presbyterian Form of Church Government were passed through the Assembly. The gist of these was offered to Charles in the treaty proposals at Uxbridge in 1645, after they had been approved of as a basis of Uniformity by the Scottish General Assembly in February. The final draft of the Propositions for Church Government was authorised by the English Parliament in 1648 as the 'Form of Church Government'. As the Directory for Church Government, it was brought to Scotland by Baillie and Gillespie in 1647 and placed before the Assembly along with the Propositions of 1644. It was given to a committee to consider in 1648 and 1649. It never passed the Assembly; older members objected to the power given to Kirk Sessions and the unsettled times following the death of Charles with the subsequent suppression of the Assembly prevented a final revision and approval. Even at the Revolution, this 'Directory' obtained no legal sanction, but the principles which it embodied passed into the law of the Church.

The 'Directory for Ordination' appended to the Form of Church Government is a striking example of Scottish influence at Westminster. Over against the more sacramental view of the English divines that ordination was the conveyance of a special grace, the Scots had it asserted that 'Ordination is the solemn setting apart of a person to some public Church office'. Over against the Independent view which equated election and ordination by placing ordination in the hands of the congregation or its representatives, the Directory asserts that 'Ordination is the act of a presbytery'. When Calamy and others maintained that ordination could be given without charge, the Scots, with the traditional Reformation objection to unplaced clergy, were reluctant to accept the English standpoint, so a compromise stated that 'It is agreeable to the Word of God and very expedient that such as are to be ordained ministers be designed to some particular Church or other ministerial charge'.

The manner and method of electing a minister was left undetermined. On this, the Scots themselves were divided. Rutherfurd believed that the right to elect vested in the congregation. Henderson was not convinced of this and even Gillespie hesitated to affirm it. Many of the English Presbyterians were opposed to any such dogma. The Independents were all for it. A formula was evolved which gave the congregation some right in the business. 'No man shall be ordained a minister for a particular congregation if they can show just cause of exception against him.' No matter was later to cause more strife in the Kirk. Rutherfurd saw his dogma made law in 1649. It continued to be law after the Revolution till the Act of 1712 placed the election of ministers again in the hands of the patrons; even the right to object became a dead letter. The Disruption split the Kirk; abolition of patronage and the restoration of popular election re-effected a Union. Yet the problem does not seem entirely solved even today.

When the main propositions on Church government were framed, the Assembly turned its attention to Public Worship. The Directory for the Public Worship of God is the most Scottish of all the Westminster standards. Scottish influence was at its highest both politically and ecclesiastically when it was framed and the Scots themselves penned much of the Directory. They had to get rid of the hated Liturgy but they were well aware of the need of an orderly form of service both as an intrinsic part of worship and as a check to the prolix and chaotic observances which were becoming common in England and threatening to appear in Scotland. The Directory was pushed through the Assembly with surprising speed which was aided perhaps by the puritan cast of mind of all the members. Its drafting was originally given not to the Assembly's Committees but to the Grand Committee perhaps because this committee included a good number of laymen and the Scots hoped for a greater anti-liturgical feeling among them than among the clerical members, some of whom had still a love for the old Book of Common Prayer. Eventually Parliament placed the framing of the Directory in the Assembly's hands. At first progress was slow; for some reason or other the Independents imagined themselves slighted and were inclined to be obstructive. More and more of the work passed into the hands of the Scots; the prayers for the Sabbath day, the directory for the Sacraments, the revision of the directory for Catechising and the directory for Preaching. Hardly a clause escaped their searching eye or reforming hand. As a pithy instruction for preaching the directory they framed is unrivalled.

Not all of the business, however, went the way of the Scots. They were unsuccessful in having their Communion practices established in the directory for the Sacrament of the Lord's Supper. The English divines were opposed to the traditional Scottish practice of sitting all together at one table, and, where there were too many to sit at one, of coming in successive companies to sit down; they were opposed also to the minister speaking words of exhortation while the elements were being partaken. The Scottish practice originally set forth in the Book of Discipline as 'convenient' had become almost integral in the celebration and a formula had ultimately to be achieved which satisfied both sides. The table was to be arranged so that 'the communicants may orderly sit about it or at it'. It was directed that the exhortation should come after the people had communicated and the Scots acquiesced for the sake of uniformity but let it be understood that each minister should do as he thought best in the matter. There were two reasons for their dour insistence on what seems relatively unimportant; this Sacrament was the central act of Scottish worship; at the same time they were under pressure from the die-hard party at home to make no more concessions, though it hardly appears that they ever made very many.

On the question of the administration of the Sacrament of Baptism, the Scots were not at unity amongst themselves—they never have been. Scottish custom caused the parents to make a profession of faith at Baptism and at least repeat or assent to the Creed before the child was baptised. Henderson maintained this as the practice of all the Reformed Churches. Rutherfurd, along with the Independents, and many English divines held that parents should not be 'catechised' at this time. The age-old questions of the child's right, the parents' duty, the danger of making the Sacrament appear to function *ex opere operato* were all heatedly debated. The result was a directory leaning to Rutherfurd's view, but the necessity of the instruction of parents before Baptism was emphatically laid down and the demand for the parents' solemn promise to fulfil their duty was not intended to engender a meaningless response, which is now perhaps too often the case.

The directory for marriage gave the Scots unusual allies—the Erastians. They were opposed to any sacramental view of marriage and in this they were supported by Lightfoot and others. Scots and Erastians considered marriage a civil contract solemnised by the Church because it entailed many religious duties. Most of the Puritans had no difficulty in accepting this doctrine though one or two of them held that there was something sacramental in the marriage ceremony. It was explicitly stated that marriage was not a sacrament. Other minor directories show the same traces of modification or control by Scottish hands. The *tout ensemble* is much nearer the Scottish conception of Public Worship than the Anglican. The order for divine service itself which is embodied in the directories for Assembling the Congregation, Public Reading of Holy Scriptures, Prayer before Sermon, Prayer after Sermon, follows with minor differences that are set forth in Henderson's *Government and Order*, which was based on Knox's Liturgy—the position of the prayers being the only essential difference. When the Directory was sanctioned by the General Assembly, the Scottish practices of sitting at the Lord's Table, of the exhortation during the partaking and of the congregation singing a psalm whilst different companies were changing seats at the table were enjoined to be kept. Whatever its merits or its ultimate fate, the General Assembly of 1645 believed with finality that their Commissioners had given them the Directory they had wanted and desired.

THE PSALMS

A note may be added on the composition of the Metrical Psalms which became as much part of the life of the Scottish Kirk as the Confession's theology. The friends of Francis Rous sought the Assembly's imprimatur on his metrical version of the Psalms as a means of helping an 'old most honest member of the House of Commons'. The Scots, at first suspicious, came to regard the project with affection and Baillie was their chief agent in following the revision of Rous's version through the Assembly. That so many psalms are in common metre is due to the Scots, for with the practical end in view, they realised that a people who loved ballad would sing psalms more readily in a stanza akin to the ballad stanza. Poetaster and Hebraist waged warfare over the various renderings, the Scots compared them with their own metrical versions and sought home advice on the matter, till, after various comings and goings, the Assembly approved a much amended version in November 1645, which the House of Commons licensed in 1646. The Lords, in a huff, because the Assembly refused to sanction also the Psalms of their candidate for psalmody honours, a Mr Barton, refused to give their sanction to the version. The Metrical Psalms came before the General Assembly in 1647 and were remitted to a committee for study and revision. After much examination and revision in committee, they were finally, in November 1649, approved by the Commission of Assembly and appointed to be printed and published for the public use. No other Westminster production had such rigorous scrutiny and certainly the Scottish emendations, due largely to Zachary Boyd, show some decided improvements on the Westminster text. Scotland received the Metrical Psalms with caution and maintained them for centuries with defiant affection.

K

CHAPTER XI

THE THEOLOGY OF THE ASSEMBLY

IT IS not possible here to enter into every dogma and aspect of the Westminster theology; but only to consider its nature and shape. After the establishment of Calvinism as the prime theology, in Scotland by Knox, in England by Cartwright, there was a native development in both these countries toward modification of the central dogma of absolute predestination. All the great Calvinists were supralapsarians, that is to say they held that God's original plan concerning the nature and destiny of man included, from the very first, the Fall and all its awful consequences of sin and death. The choice of the elect and the reprobate was implicit in God's first intention and decree. Sin was considered as a non-entitive condition, fore-ordained by God, by which the glory of His justice and mercy was showed forth and it was denied resolutely that God was, by their doctrine, made the author of sin in man. As Professor Mitchell has pointed out, there was a tradition of Augustinianism in the Anglo-Norman Church descending from Anselm and Bradwardine that aided the growth of Calvinist theology in the English universities. But there were some who felt that, while they could accept the main Calvinist doctrines, the position of the supralapsarian was too daring a speculation, and perhaps too dangerous a conjecture into the mind of God, and that not all the subtleties of Ramean philosophy and logic could sufficiently clear that doctrine of the charge that it made God the author of sin. So in Scotland and in England a native school of infralapsarians grew up, in line certainly with similar thought on the Continent, but not the result of it, for it was much later that Dutch and French works of theology began to flow across the channel, and that scholars such as Cameron and Boyd, returning from the continental universities, began to make their influence felt. The infralapsarian held as reverently as the supra-lapsarian the central doctrine of the sovereignty of God. But he considered the Fall and sin as already permitted by God and the decrees of election and reprobation as starting from the Fall as an effected fact. God out of the *massa damnota* elected some and rejected others. A further attempt at modification was made in the tentative assertion of the doctrine of praeterition by which God was held to have chosen some and passed over the others. (Attempts have been made to claim Calvin as an infralapsarian because of the part he played in drawing up the infralapsarian French Confession but he signed the Geneva Consensus which is supralapsarian and always rejected the idea that God permitted anything he did not will. Beza, his most intimate disciple, was supralapsarian and his master must be held as of the same school.) In Scotland, Robert Rollock, first Principal of Edinburgh University, was about the first to draw away from the high Calvinist position, not so much by a positive statement of infralapsarian doctrine as by his exclusive pre-occupation with God's dealings with fallen man in his treatise *De Vocatione Efficaci*. He calls the elect 'those whom he knew from eternity and predestinated unto life', which at least leaves the timing of the decree of election an open question. Andrew Melville also was an infralapsarian as is manifested in his Commentary on Romans and his theological standpoint was confirmed by his exile in France, where such views prevailed. In his preaching his pupil, Robert Bruce, revealed the same tendency. England showed the same trend of ecclesiastical thought. Barret, a Fellow of Caius, and Baro, Margaret Professor of Divinity at Cambridge, went as far as to assert that sin was the cause of reprobation. More and more the theologians drew into milder ways developing the 'Covenant' or 'Federal' theology which was primarily concerned with God's dealings with created man. Some like Davenant beginning from the infralapsarian position came to accept the 'hypothetical universalism' of Amyraut (*vide infra*), others like Andrews, by their own judgement and nature became 'Arminian' yet knew little or nothing of Arminius.

It was the advent of the Dutch scholar Arminius and his even more thoroughgoing disciples, such as Episcopius, that tore the theology of the Reformed Church in two. The cardinal doctrines of their creed were a protest against absolute predestination, against limitation of the atonement of Christ and against the doctrine of the assured state of the true believer. They held:

1. That God by an unchangeable and eternal decree in Christ, before the existence of the world, determined to elect from fallen mankind those who through His grace believe in Christ and preserve a faith and obedience, and did also resolve to reject the unbelieving and disobedient to eternal damnation.

2. Consequently Christ died for every man and by his death on the cross obtained pardon for sin for all men, but only the faithful and believing could enjoy this reconciliation and pardon.

3. Man could not obtain saving faith by his own free will but needed God's grace through Christ to be renewed in thought and will.

4. This grace was the cause of the beginning, course and completion of man's salvation. None could believe or persevere in faith without this co-operating grace; all good works must be ascribed to the grace of God in Christ. This grace, however, was not irresistible.

5. It was questioned whether a true believer could fall from grace and finally decided that he could.

These doctrines were set forth in the Remonstrance of the Dutch 'Arminians', drawn up at Gouda in 1610 by Uitenbogaert, one of the ablest of their number. Division spread in the ranks of the Dutch Reformed Church and the controversy raged in the lecture rooms of France and Holland. The theses of the Remonstrance were finally condemned at the Synod of Dort in 1619, whose 'canons' set forth a carefully worded statement of infralapsarian Calvinism.

Attempts were made before and after the Synod to form a reconciling theology which, without going as far as the Arminians, would emphasise the saving work of Christ for all men without diminishing in any way the absolute sovereignty of God. The Father of this movement was John Cameron, Professor of Divinity at Saumur, who was also between 1622 and 1626 Principal of Glasgow University, before his return to France. His views were extensively developed by his pupil, Moses Amyraut, with whose name they became associated as Amyraldism. Amyraut maintained that, along with the actual decrees of particular election and reprobation, there was a universal will of grace which was unapplied because of the sin and apostasy of fallen man. This will of grace remained in the divine idea. Christ's death was sufficient for all, but not applied or available to all, because so many were reprobate. The doctrine was really a speculative attempt to soften supralapsarian dogma and introduce—if hypothetically—the quality of mercy into the 'horrible decree'. It was condemned in the Swiss Formula Consensus of 1675 but found many supporters in England. Davenant and Ward, the English theologians at Dort, were inclined to its support and Heylin claims that James VI himself instructed them not to oppose the article of Universal Redemption.

In Britain, within Scotland and England, the theological situation soon became involved with the political. As a reaction to Arminianism, native or imported, the severer Puritans returned to the supralapsarian position which some had never left and which was a natural descendant of Anglo-Norman Augustinianism. Their great protagonist was William Twisse. The more moderate held to infralapsarianism, even to Amyraldian views. Laud and the 'High Church' party adopted the Arminian theology. Its choice by a man like Andrews was easy to understand, but what took Laud to it? A Puritan in his own way, one would have thought that predestination would have appealed to him as a better support for the sovereignty of kings. In Holland Calvinism upheld the monarchy and Barneveld, the Republican, was executed four days after the Canons of Dort were passed. As the Genevan representative remarked, 'The Canons of Dort shot off the Advocate's head.' But Laud's greatest opponents were Calvinists, and being Calvinists, Presbyterian or Independent, and the deeper their Calvinism, the greater was their opposition to him. Political considerations as well as others may have taken him to the newer creed. He may have even hoped by its introduction to disrupt the unity of Presbyterian and Puritan opposition. He failed, because if the Puritan was opposed to Arminianism theologically, he was doubly opposed to it as the creed of Laud. In Scotland, whatever chance Arminianism had of being considered on its own merits was completely demolished by the fact that it became the creed of the leaders of the Episcopal party, who were regarded as Laud's tools.

In all this complicated political theological situation one might note two bodies of men who held Arminian or semi-Arminian views induced by their own studies, and completely detached from the political situation, though one of these bodies did, in the end, become embroiled in the Scottish Revolution. There is a curious similarity in the intellectual standpoint of the Cambridge Platonists and the Aberdeen Doctors. At Cambridge men like More, Whichcote and Cudworth came to a more liberal theology through their study of ancient philosophy with little reference to continental or national controversy. In Aberdeen Dr John Forbes and his colleagues in the University sought to achieve something of the same freedom by an unbiased study of biblical sources and less reference to ecclesiastical systems. Their sincere but not bigoted adherence to Episcopacy was the cause of their dismissal at the time of the Covenant.

With theological controversy the main intellectual pre-occupation of the time, the first task to which the Westminster divines addressed themselves, was the revision of the Thirty-Nine Articles of the Church of England. As Arminianism had become the creed of the High Churchman, they aimed at bringing the Articles more in line with the 'Lambeth Articles' or with the 'Irish Articles' drawn up by Archbishop Ussher. These latter were more Calvinist in doctrine and the Irish Articles was indeed used as a basis for the subsequent Confession of Faith. The Arminians were with the King at Oxford; the Calvinists with a sprinkling of a few Amyraldians and some purely exegetical scholars held the day at

Westminster. Apart from the Cambridge Platonists, the Calvinists were England's greatest scholars and men of international repute for English Arminianism was political rather than scholarly and its greatest exponents, John Goodwin the Independent, and Helwisse the Baptist, were not Episcopalians. When the Scots arrived the divines were engaged upon the Thirty-Nine Articles but as questions of government and worship were deemed more important because of the political situation, this work was shelved till the standards of government and worship were completed.

It was not till May 1646 that, pressed by the Scots and speeded by Parliament, the divines began to formulate a Confession of Faith. After several false starts the task was finally put in the hands of a drafting committee. This committee collected all that had been done and arranged and ordered the 'heads' to be brought before the Assembly and its three main committees. After these had passed through the committees and the Assembly, they were returned to the drafting committee for final correcting and accurate wording. The Scots acted as individual theologians, but with access to all committees they had a full say in all that was determined. Actually, despite the elaborate machinery, the Confession was the work of a score of the leading theologians of the Assembly. Twisse was dead, but Rutherfurd, Seaman and Arrowsmith stoutly upheld his theology. Gattaker, Herle, Calamy, Burgess, Reynolds, Wallis and others ably scrutinised and drafted the Confession. Perhaps they looked upon it as a test of orthodoxy as much as a Confession of Faith, to the Scots it was also an instrument of ecclesiastical unity for the two nations, but the result was the greatest credal statement of post-Reformation Calvinism. Debates were keen but free from acrimony for on the whole the difference did not centre so much in the content of a doctrine as in the method of stating it. The attitude of the Assembly to the four prevailing systems of theology soon became clear. It was to anathematise Arminianism to ostracise Amyraldism, and to find a convenient formula to embrace both the supralapsarian and infralapsarian standpoint. The lengthiest debates were in chapters I, III, VIII, XX and XXIII of the Confession—Holy Scripture, God's Eternal Decree, Christ the Mediator, Christian Liberty and the Civil Magistrate—and accurately reflected the dominant theological and ecclesiastical questions of the day and the, mostly unvarying, Puritan answers to them.

The Confession follows closely the Irish Articles on which it was based, both in scheme and matter. The first chapter, like the first article, deals with Holy Scripture. Most previous reformed Confessions began with the doctrine of God, His decrees and Providence. By placing Holy Scripture first in schematic order the divines emphasised the authoritative source of their doctrine as opposed to all Roman or Anglican appeals to tradition. Parliament showed the same reverence for Scriptural authority for they later ordered that the Scriptural 'proofs' be appended to every chapter of the Confession. Actually the doctrine of God and that of Holy Scripture were formulated contemporaneously in the Assembly's committees but the scheme of the Irish Articles as indicated gave 'Holy Scripture' first place, though theologically one might have expected so Calvinist an Assembly to place the doctrine of God and His decrees in the forefront. In this post-Reformation age of superfine apologetic and controversy, the divines perhaps felt themselves bound to define first and foremost the authoritative source of all knowledge including the knowledge of God Himself. The doctrine set forth is the Reformed doctrine of the sufficiency, authority and infallibility of Holy Writ. Its canon is defined and its adequacy under the guidance of the Holy Spirit to determine all matters of faith and conduct is asserted. As Schaff writes, 'No other Protestant symbol has such a clear, judicious, concise and exhaustive statement of this fundamental article of Protestantism.'

Is the Confession infralapsarian or supralapsarian? The measure of its success as a theological formula can be judged by the fact that it is possible to claim that it is either or both. Professor J. F. Mitchell thinks that even the Amyraldian view is not excluded, though in the opinion of the present writer it most definitely was (*vide infra*). As in the Canons of Dort, the pervasive theology is infralapsarian, so in the Westminster Confession it is supra-lapsarian though it is so carefully worded that the infralapsarian could subscribe without offence. The third chapter of God's Eternal Decree asserts the doctrine of absolute predestination from all Eternity. Seamen, a resolute supralapsarian, sought to have the truth driven brutally home to the reprobate by adding the words 'in the same decree' to the phrase 'and others fore-ordained to everlasting death'. But as this was implied in the heading itself, Rutherfurd, the greatest supralapsarian of them all, thought it unnecessary and the connective 'so' was used. Thus the chapter runs:

(1) God from all eternity did, by the most wise and holy council of his own will, freely and unchangeably ordain what-soever comes to pass; yet so, as thereby neither is God the author of sin, nor is violence offered to the will of the creatures, nor is the liberty or contingency of second causes taken away, but rather established.

(2) Although God knows whatsoever may or can come to pass upon all supposed conditions; yet hath he not decreed anything because he foresaw it as future, or as that which would come to pass on such conditions.

(3) By the decree of God, for the manifestation of his Glory, some men and angels are predestinated unto everlasting life, and others fore-ordained to everlasting death.

To this the infralapsarian could subscribe, but the whole logic is the logic of the supralapsarian. Indeed the infralapsarian position is in reality a refusal to take the final step back in theo-logical argument through fear of being thought to make God the author of sin; a charge to which the supralapsarian found many highly speculative answers. In the same debate the divines turned down the Amyraldian views of Calamy and Vines who tried to have some clause deepening the worth of Christ's sacrifice added to the phrase 'Neither are any other redeemed by Christ—but the elect only', but even the phrase used at Dort 'sufficiently for all' was ruled out and Christ was logically held to have died for the elect only. They rejected also the doctrine of mere praeterition, that God passed by the non-elect, and adamantly insisted on 'fore-ordained to everlasting death'. It has been held that 'fore-ordained' is a little milder than 'predestinated' but there would seem little difference either in intention or result in the two terms. Nowhere is it stated in words that God decreed the Fall, or ordained to permit the Fall as some supralapsarians put it; the most of the Confession is content with the infralapsarian perspective of man as fallen and goes on from there, but none reading the first three chapters can deny the supralapsarian implications of the doctrine there stated which are further emphasised by the apologetic clauses on the authorship of sin and freedom of the will. It is impossible to be a Calvinist without being ultimately a supralapsarian and impossible to be a supralapsarian without denying vigorously that your doctrine makes God the author of sin.

When they came to consider God's dealings with created man the divines adopted, one might almost say initiated, the 'federal theology', for at Westminster this doctrine first emerges in Confessional form. It had not appeared systematically stated in any previous Confession and is glossed upon in the Irish Articles. Bullinger, however, had made use of the federal or 'covenant' scheme which was afterwards taught in England by Peter Martyr at Oxford, Martin Bucer at Cambridge and John Alasco in London. By the time of the Assembly there was a growing native literature on the subject of which the most noted work was John Ball's treatise of the Covenant of Grace published in 1645, four years after his death, and in the same year as the *Marrow of Modern Divinity*, also a 'federal' treatise. This Covenant theology finds classic utterance in Chapter VII of the Confession especially in the second and third paragraphs which run:

II. The first covenant made with man was a covenant of works, wherein life was promised to Adam, and in him to his posterity, upon condition of perfect and personal obedience.

III. Man by his fall having made himself incapable of life by that covenant, the Lord was pleased to make a second, commonly called the Covenant of Grace: whereby he freely offereth unto sinners life and salvation by Jesus Christ, requiring of them faith in him, that they may be saved; and promising to give unto those that are ordained unto life his Holy Spirit, to make them willing and able to believe.

The doctrine was little disputed in the Assembly and became a theological commonplace for over two centuries and was developed on the Continent into a full-blown theological system by Cocceius shortly after the Confession appeared. The divines were predisposed to accept this federal theology for the works of Ball and Fisher had just been published and were immensely popular. Again the whole idea of 'Covenant' enmeshed and enthralled them. They knew of the National Covenant between men of one faith to free their nation; they were sworn to the Solemn League and Covenant, a pledge between neighbour nations. The political philosophers of the Parliament side talked much of the Covenant between the King and the people, deriving their doctrine largely from the monarchomachs of France and Holland. It was inevitable that the members of the Assembly should state the relationship of God and man in covenant terms; in more ways than as a reaction to Arminianism or to Episcopacy the standards of the Assembly were influenced by the political thinking of the time. In Scotland the Covenant theology took immediate and firm hold. Rutherfurd published his *Covenant of Life Opened* and almost at the same time appeared *The Sum of Saving Knowledge* by Dickson and Durham, while the later works of Boston of Ettrick and the Marrow controversy further entrenched this theology in Scottish thought.

As the opening chapters of the Confession outline boldly and resonantly the purpose of God and the plan of His working, so the succeeding chapters fill out that plan with a comprehensive and dignified statement of Reformed soteriology. Again to quote Schaff, 'Chapters X-XVIII contain the best confessional statement of the evangelical doctrines of justification, adoption,

sanctification, saving faith, good works and assurance of salvation.' Just sometimes the wording savours of the therapeutic
handbook but it is always careful and reasoned, never trite.
Reference has already been made to the doctrine of the redemptive
work of Christ found in the Confession. In Chapter III the doctrine
of Calvinist particularism is explicitly stated: 'Neither are any other
redeemed by Christ . . . but the elect only.' Professor A. F.
Mitchell, reviewing the phraseology of later chapters, holds,
somewhat tentatively, that the doctrine of hypothetical universalism—that Christ died sufficiently and potentially for all, though
in effect only for the elect—is to be found in the Confession.
Schaff in measure adheres to his view, writing, 'On the other
hand Chapter VII teaches that under the Covenant of Grace the
Lord "freely offereth unto sinners life and salvation by Jesus
Christ, requiring of them faith in him, that they may be saved;
and promising to give unto them that are ordained unto life his
Holy Spirit, to make them willing and able to believe". This
looks like a compromise between conditional universalism taught
in the first clause and particular election taught in the second.
This is the substance of the theory of the school of Saumar—
which was afterwards condemned in the Helvetic Consensus
Formula (1675).' It only 'looks like a compromise', if indeed it
does that. The word is 'sinners' and not 'all' and is qualified by
'those that are ordained unto life' and we are still confronted by
the first and final statement, 'but the elect only'. The Assembly
debates show that the great majority of the divines were determined to exclude any Amyraldian interpretation from the Confession. McLeod Campbell, who first believed such an interpretation, was included, finally came to conclude that it was not—but
neither is the view that the elect are a select band of the very few.

The rest of the Confession deals with Church, State and Sacraments. Regarding the latter, it now seems surprising with what
little debate the chapters were framed. The doctrines of the Lord's
Supper is the common Reformed doctrine of all the Confessions,
asserting clearly the spiritual presence of the Redeemer. There
was no difference of any import between Anglican and Puritan

over it, for it was the common doctrine of Cranmer, Hooker, Ussher, Knox, Twisse and Rutherfurd. Only in later years did the great sacramental gulf between Anglican and Presbyterian become so steeply fixed. On the matter of the Church the Protestant distinction of the Church Invisible and the Church Visible is clearly stated and tersely and historically explained and the headship of Christ unambiguously and unreservedly asserted. In the matter of Church and State the divines neither sought nor constructed any compromise formula. 'There is no other head of the Church than the Lord Jesus Christ.' Pope, Prince, Prelate or Parliament were all excluded from sharing that Headship. It was the formulation of this doctrine which, as we have seen, brought the divines into bitter conflict with Parliament. When eventually the Confession was approved by Parliament as 'Articles of the Christian Religion' lip service was paid to the doctrine by keeping Chapter XXV in which it was stated, but Chapter XXX (of Church Censures), Chapter XXXI (of Synods and Councils), Chapter XX (of Christian Liberty) and sections of Chapter XXIV (of Marriage and Divorce) were all omitted because they gave either too much power to the Church or too little control to the Magistrate. The entire Confession of Faith was approved by Assembly and Estates in Scotland in 1649, invalidated by the Act Recissory of 1661 but finally approved at the Revolution in 1690.

The Westminster Confession is Protestantism's greatest complement and compliment to John Calvin. No other Confession so firmly, fully and felicitously states the cardinal doctrines of his teaching. It speedily became the classic exposition of Calvinism for the English-speaking world. It has its defects. Although it places the doctrine of Holy Scripture first in order, the doctrines of the Confession centre on that of the Eternal Decree for as Schaff has pointed out 'it makes the predestinarian scheme control the historical and christological'. That being so the ultimate inference is that the Confession is supralapsarian in theology and God's judgement rather than His love is found emphasised as the means of his revealing His Glory, but we have ample evidence also that these divines could teach and preach grandly of the love of God, and in persecution die still believing in it. Were they 'wrong' in their theology? Who can say? Modern theology may have removed the Fall to a parabolic background but the thinking Christian has still his problems of predestination and these can yet only find an answer in the nature of God Himself.

After they had formulated the Confession the Assembly proceeded to draft the Larger and Shorter Catechisms. In this work the Scots had little part, for all but Rutherfurd had gone home. The Catechisms contained the essence of the Confession and both were approved by the Assembly and adopted as teaching manuals of the Church of Scotland in 1648. The Shorter Catechism has been claimed as unsurpassed 'in beauty, terseness and accuracy of definition' and through its less metaphysical and anthropological and soteriological teaching, the federal theology of Westminster was made the working faith of the Scottish people, while the Psalms became the outlet of their vocal religious emotions.

The High Calvinism of Westminster was, as far as England was concerned, the peak of her Augustinian tradition; thereafter that tradition waned. An Amyraldian theology prevailed through Baxter and the Calamys in the oppressed nonconformist Church. Later English Presbyterianism became almost synonymous with Unitarianism until the revival and resuscitation of the Presbyterian Church of England under Scottish influence. In Scotland after the Revolution of 1690 the Confession became the doctrinal standard of the Church and the test of orthodoxy till, on a later day, the modifying clause was added to the oath of subscription. The Church was drawn from a milder form of Calvinist and Augustinian doctrine to one, harder, more rigid and logical in scheme, from which to break away was heresy. The theology of the Marrow Men, for example, was condemned because it seemed to imply the doctrine of 'hypothetical universalism' in the federal relationship between God, Christ and Man. But stern as this teaching was, it perpetuated the Reformed dogma and tradition in the Scottish Church with the sovereignty of God as its dominating principle.

CHAPTER XII

CONCLUSION

WITH THE DEATH of Rutherfurd and the execution of Guthrie and Argyll the sun set on the Covenanting parties and the night, for them, lasted nearly thirty years. Episcopacy was re-established and the recalcitrant and rebellious suppressed by the doughty deeds of Dalziel, Grierson and Claverhouse who brutally carried out the wishes of a cynical King and his successive and successively dissolute Commissioners and not unnaturally begot as fierce and murderous a spirit in some of their opponents. But Presbyterianism survived all these things and emerged chastened but triumphant at the Revolution, survived of itself and not merely because of a political act of William of Orange, although William with Carstares at his right hand undoubtedly supported the Presbyterian cause because of the Episcopalian allegiance to James. Nobody can accurately assess the relative numbers of Presbyterians and Episcopalians in Scotland in 1690. It certainly was not two Episcopalians to one Presbyterian[1]; it may have been the other way about for the Lowlands were more populous than the north. The north-east was Episcopal; the south-west was fanatically Presbyterian; mid-Scotland was Presbyterian in worship, discipline and sympathy, accepted the bishop with resignation and saw him leave with no regret. Nobody could regret the disappearance of the Highland Host, 'a rabble of caterans accustomed to murder and theft', or the disbanding of Dalziel's ruffians; Cromwell's army of occupation left a fairer name than these kindly Scots. The discipline of the Kirk Session may have been sometimes an ill-judged and vexatious thing, but it was not the

---

[1] Based on a letter of General Mackay obviously written to prevent his Presbyterian friends spoiling their case by over-reaching themselves in their demands

discipline of torture, exile and the gibbet. In power the Presbyterian had been harsh and vindictive, but he had never applied
the boot or trafficked in white slavery by selling his compatriots
to the Americas. There were many reasons why people were
glad to see Presbyterianism back and the Presbyterianism that
came back was the Presbyterianism fashioned between 1638
and 1650.

Popular history not infrequently fastens on salient truth more
accurately than reams of research, and 'Jenny Geddes's' stool is, in
a way, a symbol of the whole revolution. In its popular aspect
the upheaval of 1638 was a continuance of the Reformation revolt
against 'idolatry' in worship, started in Scotland by Knox, which
had shown some regrettable excesses, but as Froude writes,
'Suppose the Kirk had been the broad, liberal, philosophical intellectual thing which some people think it ought to have been,
how would it have fared in that crusade; how altogether would it
have encountered those surplices of Archbishop Laud or those
Dragoons of Claverhouse. . . . For more than half a century the
battle had to be fought out in Scotland, which in reality was the
battle between liberty and despotism. . . . The Covenanters
fought the fight and won the victory, and then, and not till then,
came the David Humes with their essays on miracles, and the
Adam Smiths with their political economics, and steam engines
and railroads and philosophical institutions and all the blessed or
unblessed fruits of liberty.'[1] The first-fruits of the victory was
the establishment of a Puritan worship which persisted throughout
the Restoration regime and continued for centuries afterwards.
The literary agent of this establishment was the 'Directory for the
Public Worship of God'. There is no need to go into the question
of how far it was followed in every detail by the Church which
adopted it or to compare it here, favourably or unfavourably,
with other Scottish liturgies. Drafted in England, it was an
eminently Scottish production which maintained a Puritan worship in Scotland and achieved the positive ends aimed at by the
somewhat negative criticism of 'Jenny Geddes's' stool-throwing.

---

[1] *Short Studies on Great Subjects* 1, 180

Hymns and the 'nocent ceremonies' and other assets of order and beauty are now found in her service, but the worship of the Church of Scotland in intelligent simplicity and scriptural dignity remains the Puritan worship of a Reformed Church.

The 'Second Reformation' created in the system of courts set out in the 'Form and Order of Church Government', the form of Church government to which we are now accustomed. The final draft of this formulary never became law in the Church, although many of its propositions were sanctioned by the General Assembly in 1645. As was seen, disputes over the nature of the Kirk Session as a separate court of the Church held up such sanction in the Assemblies of 1649 and this formulary was laid aside in the troublous times that followed. Nevertheless in these times the parochial and ecclesiastical power of the Kirk Session became surely established, in fact and deed, as well as in theory. The abolition of the National Assembly by Cromwell and Charles perhaps even strengthened their power in determining local parochial affairs. The 'lay' element in her courts had been of supreme service to the Church of the Covenant in her dealings with the body politic and this period saw the elder firmly instituted as a necessary component of all her assemblies. At the Revolution, although the 'Form and Order' was not brought forward and sanctioned, its ecclesiastical system was gradually and tacitly accepted as that of the Church. During the years between 1638 and 1649 the General Assembly re-acquired its distinctive and national character. It became a power in the land as great as Parliament and the two bodies were closely knit because many of the members of the Estates were, as elders, members of Assembly also. The right was asserted and kept of dealing with all Church affairs independent of the sovereign power of the State. At the Revolution this right was in measure encroached upon—but only in measure; as Charles II learned from the fate of his father that there were liberties which he could not destroy and policies he dare not openly pursue, so the State—even an English Parliament—came to learn limits to its meddling in the Scottish Church. Realising, for instance, the explosion which would arise from any interference with the doctrine or government of the Church, but wishing to gain control of its ministers, a Union Parliament in 1712 reintroduced patronage and, undoing the work of Rutherfurd, confirmed at the Revolution, instituted the condition which caused the Disruptions. But in doctrine, worship, government and discipline the Church in the main was left supreme in her own house. In 1693-94 the Assembly courageously defended its right to convene itself and settled the matter for all time in a practice which does give it that right. In 1697 the Barrier Act whose principles Rutherfurd had long maintained was passed. As time went on the dagger thrusts aimed at her heart were succeeded by vexatious pinpricks thrust into her body, though the Church was none the worse of being bled of intolerance of her neighbours.

To Henderson and his colleagues we owe the practical establishment of the Commission of Assembly. Half court and half committee, it was regarded by many with fear and suspicion that it might be the means of delivering the Kirk over to the control of a few, but it was imperative that there should be a body of churchmen who could meet speedily to deal with each emergency as it arose and so the Commission came into being. Baillie wrote in 1643, 'The Commission from the General Assembly which before was of small use is like to become almost a constant judicatory and very profitable.'[1] Its powers and functions may have varied and altered, but it has become a vital adjunct of the Presbyterian system.

The reaction against Arminianism gave Scotland a harder theology than that which might normally have developed and the later influence of Turretin did nothing to soften the strain. The Westminster Confession became a test of orthodoxy and the way of the rebel was hard. Slowly, very slowly did the Church learn tolerance in doctrinal matters, yet one sometimes wonders if a church which has only one sort of theology is in any worse case than a church which has every sort. Social accusations have been levelled time and again at the theology of these Covenanters.

[1] Baillie, *Letters* ii, 55

It is claimed that it made them a cruel and bloodthirsty lot, as witness their witch-hunts and, of course, Philiphaugh. Witch-hunts were as common in England as in Scotland and the treatment of the unfortunate victims as cruel; they were a good long road older than Calvinist theology. The Church's attitude in Scotland was the unfortunate attitude of all Churches of the age, who in this shared an inherited Judaism. Can military atrocities be attributed to theological and ideological causes? It has always seemed to me that race, revenge and loot play the biggest part in their perpetration. In the last war and in any war the justification of a hideous or inhumane method has been 'the other side began it'. In England and in Scotland the Cavalier party were the first to unleash indiscriminate brutality. Rupert's sack of Bolton and Montrose's of Aberdeen were the first acts of their kind in the two countries. With them and the Ulster Massacre in their mind the Lowland Scots sought revenge on the perpetrators of these frightfulnesses, adding at Philiphaugh another to the number. In credit to both Scots and English these doings were few compared to the Continental holocausts. In Scotland atrocities began with James Graham's sack of Aberdeen and ended with John Graham's murders and confiscations in the Galloway hills and the Gallovidian Stair's revenge at Glencoe. Graham's known rapacity had a lot more to do with his conduct than his Arminianism and Stair's policy and the clan feuds of the Campbells much more to do with the latter than their Calvinism. Ideology may start a war but human passions dictate the way of its waging.

It is said that Westminster Calvinism frustrated or destroyed Scottish culture. What culture? Calvinists have had their literary triumphs, the translation of the 'Authorised Version' and *The Pilgrim's Progress* among them. Poets and writers from John Milton to John Buchan have owed much to the Puritan tradition in which they were reared though in their writings there may be some departure from and criticism of it. It can hardly be a reproach to Scottish Calvinism that in the midst of a bitter struggle for life it produced little great verse, nor that a Congreve or a Suckling are not found in its ranks. In the diaries of the seventeenth century there is enough racy Scots prose to delight the heart of any Scottish nationalist and in the sermons of the time there are passages of vivid description and pawky Scots epigrams sufficient to show that the literary instinct of the Scot was not dead. If we have no great drama we can think with pride of the economists, mathematicians, agriculturalists, engineers, surgeons, philosophers, theologians, novelists and preachers nourished in a Calvinist tradition who preserved us from being a futile provincial Athens —without the former glory of that great city state and gave us a greater and more varied culture than that of nostalgic historians and literary dilettantes. The Calvinist Scot despite the narrowness of his theology was the most educated peasant of his time. If his achievements are taken out of the records of the eighteenth and nineteenth centuries the history of the British Commonwealth will show many wide gaps. Native genius and hardihood accounts for much but as much was due to the stern faith in which he was reared.

The Covenants not only changed the political and religious system in Scotland, they altered the destiny of Britain and Europe. When Cromwell lay unhorsed and dazed at Marston Moor and Rupert charged aimlessly after Leven, Crawfurd rallied the fort and David Leslie poured in with the Scottish horse to win the day for the Puritan cause and ultimately for a Protestant Britain. Marston Moor was the turning point in the Civil War and but for the Scots it might well have been lost to Parliament. The Scottish Covenanters that day gave England the political freedom which neither the cunning of the second Charles nor the folly of the second James could ruin.

INDEX